Money Hacks

Forbidden Money Behind Closed Doors (That's Why You're Reading This)

Jett Thompson

Journey Together LTD

Copyright © 2025 by Journey Together LTD

All rights reserved.

No portion of this book may be reproduced in any form without written permission from the publisher or author, except as permitted by U.S. copyright law.

Contents

Introduction: Money Isn't Magic — It's Momentum ... 1
1. Saving Without Feeling Miserable ... 4
2. Smart Spending (Still Get the Stuff You Love) ... 11
3. Managing Debt Without Losing Your Mind ... 20
4. The Money Mindset Shift ... 29
5. Budgeting for People Who Hate Budgeting ... 38
6. Finding Hidden Money in Your Life ... 46
7. Investing Without Fear (Or FOMO) ... 53
8. Building Your Emergency Fund Without Stress ... 61
9. Mastering Everyday Money Moves ... 69
10. Lifestyle Upgrades That Don't Break the Bank ... 76
11. Resetting After a Money Mistake ... 84
12. Saving for Fun: Goals That Make You Smile ... 92
13. Financial Self-Care: Money Moves for Your Mental Health ... 100
Conclusion: Your Wins Are Already in Motion ... 107

Introduction: Money Isn't Magic — It's Momentum

If you've ever looked at your bank account, sighed dramatically, and thought, *"Maybe I should just win the lottery,"* you're not alone. Honestly, if financial success came down to luck, most of us would be stuck living off vending machine snacks by now.

Good news: it's not luck. It's not magic. And it's definitely not about turning yourself into a spreadsheet-loving robot who never leaves the house unless there's a coupon involved.

Real money wins come from momentum, not miracles.

They come from tiny moves stacked up over time, not some secret genius gene you're missing. It's not about being perfect. It's about getting just a little smarter, a little faster, and a lot funnier with how you handle money in real life. You don't need to fix yourself. **You just need better cheats.**

Welcome to the Shortcut Society. Official membership status: *already approved.*

You're not bad with money. You're not doomed. And you don't need to overhaul your entire life to start winning financially. What you *do* need is a few smarter shortcuts — the kind that slip into your regular life without feeling like punishment.

This book isn't about building perfect budgets, clipping coupons until your fingers bleed, or pretending you're thrilled to spend Saturday night batch-cooking lentils. It's about setting you up with **practical, sneaky, low-effort moves** that actually work for real humans living real lives — chaos, cravings, coffee habits, Amazon carts, and all.

There's a reason you've struggled with money in the past: **most advice is built for robots, not humans.** Humans are messy. We have good days and terrible days. We impulse-buy weird gadgets at 2 a.m. We occasionally forget to cancel free trials. *(Seriously, how many streaming services do you even have right now?)*

It's not about being broken. It's about building momentum anyway.

Momentum is what happens when you stop aiming for massive, perfect leaps and start stacking tiny wins. It's what happens when you celebrate transferring $10 to savings like you just won an Oscar. When you find hidden money you didn't even know was leaking. When you finally breathe a little easier because you have an emergency fund that's bigger than just "hope and vibes."

Tiny moves made smarter and faster are what real financial success is built on.

You don't have to be a math genius. You don't have to quit your daily coffee. You don't have to live like a monk.

You just need to keep showing up for yourself in small, doable ways — and that's what we'll do together here.

Throughout this book, you're going to find smarter shortcuts for:

- Saving money without feeling like you've signed up for a life of eternal suffering.
- Spending on the stuff you love without sabotaging your future.
- Paying off debt without losing your mind (or your will to live).
- Building an emergency fund that actually gives you peace.
- Investing without getting trapped in jargon or FOMO spirals.
- Resetting after money mistakes without the shame hangover.
- Upgrading your life without upgrading your stress.

And most importantly? **You'll learn how to treat money moves like self-care, not self-punishment.**

Shortcut Society Rules to Live By:

- **Rule #1:** You don't have to do it perfectly. You just have to keep doing it.

- **Rule #2:** If it feels miserable, you're doing it wrong. *(We fix that.)*
- **Rule #3:** Celebrate every tiny win like you just slayed a dragon. *(Because you did.)*

Real financial wins aren't reserved for people who never make mistakes. They're built by people who make the next best move anyway.

You're not bad with money. **You just haven't had the right cheats yet.**

Ready to start stacking tiny wins, building real momentum, and finally feeling *good* about money without needing a miracle (or a personality transplant)? Let's go. **Shortcut Society awaits.**

Saving Without Feeling Miserable

Sneaky ways to build savings without feeling like you live on instant noodles.

Saving money gets a bad rap. Somewhere along the line, it started sounding like punishment: No fun, no coffee, no life. Just spreadsheets and sad packed lunches.

Good news: *We don't do boring or miserable around here.* Saving isn't about denial—it's about building freedom, one tiny, sneaky move at a time. You don't have to give up all the good stuff. You just need smarter systems that make your money quietly grow in the background while you keep living.

This chapter is packed with painless shortcuts that will fatten your savings without making you feel trapped in a ramen-only diet. Let's build your stash—with snacks still included.

Micro-Savings Magic – Tiny Moves, Huge Results

Saving doesn't always mean shoving $500 a month into a vault. Sometimes, it's about stacking a hundred tiny wins you barely notice. Micro-savings make it almost impossible to fail because the effort feels… basically invisible.

You'll be amazed how fast these little habits build real cash piles—and spoiler: It'll happen while you're busy living your everyday life.

- **Hack #1: Pocket Change Power**

When you buy something, round it up to the nearest $5 and stash the difference. A few bucks here and there turn into serious savings without any pain.

- **Hack #2: The $5 Bill Challenge**

Whenever a $5 bill lands in your hand, save it immediately. It feels small but stacks up fast into a surprise money mountain.

- **Hack #3: One Less Habit**

Drop one tiny daily splurge—like a $2 coffee or snack—and redirect it to savings. You won't miss it, but your bank balance will notice.

- **Hack #4: Round-Up Apps FTW**

Apps like Acorns or Revolut automatically round up your card purchases and save the change: zero effort, real results.

- **Hack #5: Secret Cash Stash Jar**

Toss your spare coins and small notes into a hidden jar. It's old-school, but shockingly effective when you check it a few months later.

The Pay-Yourself-First Trick – Get Paid, Then Hide It

You don't need willpower if you never see the money in the first place. Paying yourself first means treating savings like a bill you MUST pay, not an optional leftover.

By auto-moving even a tiny amount the second your paycheck lands, you'll trick your future self into being financially fierce, without feeling the pinch.

- **Hack #6: Auto-Transfer Ambush**

Set an automatic savings transfer to trigger the second your paycheck hits. If you never see it, you'll never spend it.

- **Hack #6: Minimum Viable Saving**

Even $10 counts. Start so small it feels silly, then bump it up a little as you get used to it.

- **Hack #8: Multiple Savings Buckets**

Name your savings goals ("Beach Trip," "New Laptop") and feed them tiny amounts regularly. Seeing the goals grow keeps you hooked.

- **Hack #9: Hidden Account Trick**

Open a savings account at a different bank with no app access. Out of sight, out of mind—and out of reach for impulse buys.

- **Hack #10: Reward Yourself for Deposits**

Treat yourself to something tiny every time you save, like a $1 chocolate bar. Savings should feel like winning, not punishment.

Secret Bank Accounts (Just for You) – Out of Sight, Growing Strong

When money is too easy to access, it tends to vanish mysteriously ("I swear I only bought coffee..."). That's why secret, hard-to-reach savings accounts are so powerful.

Treat your savings like it's on a distant island. Harder to touch = bigger chance you'll leave it alone to thrive.

- **Hack #11: Rename It Something Boring**

Call your savings account something hideous like "Dental Work Fund." You'll be way less tempted to dip into it.

- **Hack #12: Use a Different Bank**

Stash your savings at a different bank with no linked app. Friction saves fortunes.

- **Hack #13: High-Yield Side Quest**

Pick a savings account that pays actual interest—your money will grow while you forget about it.

- **Hack #14: Direct Deposit to Secret Stash**

Split part of your paycheck to go straight to the secret account. Money you never see is money you can't spend.

- **Hack #15: Only Raid for Real Emergencies**

Make strict rules: broken car = OK, Black Friday sale = NOPE.

Trick Yourself Into Saving More – Your Brain is a Sucker (Use It)

Saving isn't about being "better." It's about setting traps you actually want to fall into. Use psychological tricks to nudge yourself toward saving without feeling like you're missing out.

- **Hack #16: Save Your Raises**

Every time you get a pay raise, save the difference. In the future, you will build wealth without even noticing.

- **Hack #17: Savings Leaderboard**

Challenge friends or family to monthly savings competitions. The loser buys the next pizza.

- **Hack #18: Visual Goal Thermometers**

Draw a big savings thermometer on your wall or fridge. Watching the line go up is weirdly addictive.

- **Hack #19: Trigger Habit Trick**

Save $1 every time you check Instagram or TikTok. Your savings will grow almost as fast as your screen time.

- **Hack #20: Pay-to-Play Rule**

Buy something impulsively? Fine yourself $5 to savings. Instant money guilt turned into money gain.

Why Future You Will Thank You – Plant Trees You'll Sit Under Later

Right now, saving can feel thankless. But Future You? They're gonna build statues in your honor.

This subchapter is your pep talk to stay in the game, because what you build today matters way more than it feels in the moment.

- **Hack #21: Write a Letter to Future You**

Write a quick note to open when you hit your savings goal. Hint: make it proud and funny.

- **Hack #22: Name Your Goals Something Fun**

Call your savings accounts things like "Paris 2026" or "Freedom Fund"—names that make you want to keep feeding them.

- **Hack #23: Monthly Gratitude Check-Ins**

Once a month, look at your growing savings and high-five yourself. Pride keeps momentum alive.

- **Hack #24: Reward Every $100 Milestone**

For every $100 saved, do something nice for yourself (cheaply). Positive reinforcement works.

- **Hack #25: Dream Budget Planning**

Budget for future fun—vacations, early retirement, or "quit your job" days. The dream will drive the discipline.

Grocery Hacks That Save You Hundreds – Food, Glorious (Cheaper) Food

Groceries aren't optional—but overpaying for them is. A few clever tweaks at the store (and in your fridge) will save you serious cash without turning dinner into a punishment.

- **Hack #26: Eat Before You Shop**

Shopping hungry = buying things that your wallet and waistline regret. Always eat first.

- **Hack #27: The Half-List Hack**

Make your grocery list—and then cut it in half. You probably didn't need half of it anyway.

- **Hack #28: DIY Snack Packs**

Buy snacks in bulk and portion them yourself. Prepackaged = overpriced.

- **Hack #29: Price Per Unit Power Moves**

Always check the price per kilogram or litre, not per item. Bulk usually wins.

- **Hack #30: No-Fly Zone for Eye-Level Products**

Eye-level is where stores put the expensive stuff. Look high and low for better deals.

How to Win Tiny No-Spend Challenges – Go Broke (on Purpose) for Fun

No-spend challenges aren't about sad, boring weeks eating plain oats. They're mini-games to flex your creativity muscle—and give your wallet a breather.

You'll discover how little you actually *need* when you flip the script for a few days—and you might even have fun doing it.

- **Hack #31: The 3-Day Wallet Lockdown**

Challenge yourself to three full days of no spending (except real emergencies). You'll be shocked at how much money and willpower you have.

- **Hack #32: Zero-Dollar Weekend Adventure**

Plan a weekend packed with free fun: hikes, movie marathons, beach days. No spending is allowed, and boredom is not invited.

- **Hack #33: Pantry Party Cooking**

Eat only what's already in your fridge and pantry for a few days. It's weirdly fun and guarantees lower grocery bills next week.

- **Hack #34: Social Swap Meet**

Instead of buying stuff, swap books, clothes, or games with friends. It's like shopping, minus the painful bank notification.

- **Hack #35: No-Spend Buddy System**

Grab a partner, set the rules, and check in daily. Team challenges make it harder to cheat (and way more fun).

The Invisible Money Method – Save It Like You Never Had It

Invisible money is money you never miss because it never hits your active spending life. This subchapter will show you how to hide money from yourself so well, you'll be shocked at what you "accidentally" save.

- **Hack #36: Bank Transfer on Pay Raise Day**

Whenever you get a raise, instantly send that difference to savings. Pretend it never happened.

- **Hack #37: Found Money = Fun Split**

If you find unexpected cash (rebates, refunds, birthday money), split it 50/50 between fun and savings.

- **Hack #38: Invisible Increase Plan**

Every 6 months, raise your automatic savings

by 1% without telling yourself—slow, painless upgrade.

- **Hack #39: Pay Extra, Pocket the Difference**

If a bill goes down (like insurance or phone plan), keep paying the old amount into your savings account.

- **Hack #40: Set and Forget Success**

Automation beats willpower every time. Set savings once and let them grow silently in the background.

Smart Spending (Still Get the Stuff You Love)

How to buy what you want and still have money left to high-five yourself later.

Spending smarter isn't about living like a budgeting robot who never sees sunlight. It's about finding ways to enjoy the stuff you love without waking up to a terrifying bank statement. You don't need to quit shopping or deny yourself happiness — you just need a few clever tricks up your sleeve.

This chapter is packed with shortcuts that let you outsmart impulse buys, grab the deals that actually matter, and stretch your money like a boss. Let's flip the script so you feel like a genius every time you swipe that card.

The 24-Hour Cart Pause – Outsmart Your Impulse Brain

Impulse buying isn't evil — it's just impatient. Our brains love quick hits of happiness, and buying shiny new things delivers exactly that. But often, the high fades faster than a cheap coffee buzz, and we're left with stuff we didn't really want (and less money than we needed).

The easiest trick? Delay the decision. Giving yourself 24 hours between "I want it" and "I'm buying it" can completely change the outcome. In this section, you'll learn how patience can turn you into a spending ninja — no deprivation required.

- **Hack #41: 24-Hour Cart Pause**

When you want something, drop it in your cart and walk away for a full day. Tomorrow's you is usually better at spotting unnecessary splurges than today's you.

- **Hack #42: Cart Abandonment Bonus**

Leaving things sitting in your cart sometimes triggers discount emails from desperate brands. Winning by doing nothing? Yes, please.

- **Hack #43: Would I Buy at Double? Test**

Ask yourself: Would I still want this if it cost twice as much? If the answer is "meh," congratulations — you just saved yourself a regretful purchase.

- **Hack #44: Wishlist It, Don't Buy It**

Instead of buying immediately, add it to a wishlist. You'll either save up intentionally or realize you didn't want it that badly after all.

- **Hack #45: Save It to Pinterest**

Create a "Want" board on Pinterest and pin your shopping cravings. It scratches the itch without destroying your bank balance.

How to Build a Guilt-Free Splurge Budget – Treat Yo Self (Strategically)

The fastest way to blow up a good money plan? Total deprivation. If you try to eliminate every bit of fun, your brain eventually rebels — it usually rebels into an online shopping cart. Instead of trying to live like a monk, plan for the fun stuff. Splurging is healthy when it's part of the plan, not a random act of emotional chaos.

A guilt-free splurge budget lets you enjoy your money without the "oops" afterward. In this section, you'll learn how to carve out space for treats, celebrations, and small luxuries while still moving toward your bigger financial goals. Spoiler: You'll enjoy your splurges way more when they're on purpose.

- **Hack #46: Fun Money Fund**

Set aside a small amount every month just for fun. It's yours to spend however you want, no guilt, no judgment.

- **Hack #47: Pre-Approve Big Treats**

If you're dreaming about a bigger splurge (new phone, weekend getaway), plan for it in advance. Budget it like you would your rent.

- **Hack #48: Splurge Savings Jar**

Create a physical or digital jar where you toss small amounts whenever you can. Watching it fill up makes spending it later even sweeter.

- **Hack #49: Buy Memories, Not Just Stuff**

Whenever you splurge, lean toward experiences instead of random gadgets. Memories last longer than the thrill of ripping open a box.

- **Hack #50: Celebration Savings**

Treat yourself to a mini reward every time you hit a financial goal. Training your brain to associate saving with good things is pure genius.

Loyalty Programs That Actually Pay Off – Free Perks Without the Drama

Not all loyalty programs are just marketing fluff. Some can stack up real rewards if you use them with intention. The key is picking programs that naturally fit your normal shopping habits — not chasing points for stuff you don't need.

In this section, you'll learn how to spot the loyalty deals worth your time and stack perks without overcomplicating your life: smarter rewards, less effort, way more free coffee.

- **Hack #51: One or Two Programs Max**

Focus on one or two loyalty programs where you already spend money. Diluting your efforts across twenty programs just waters down the rewards.

- **Hack #52: Grocery and Gas Points Power**

These are places you're spending money anyway — racking up points here is free bonus cash if you remember to use your account.

- **Hack #53: Double Dip Loyalty and Cashback**

Some apps and cards let you earn loyalty points and cashback on the same transaction. It's the double scoop of financial wins.

- **Hack #54: Birthday Freebies Bonanza**

Sign up for birthday reward programs. It's free stuff just for existing another year — cake tastes better when it's free.

- **Hack #55: Set and Forget Rewards**

Link your loyalty numbers to your payment cards so you earn automatically. No remembering, no missed points, no stress.

When to Buy Used (and When Not To) – Preloved Wins and Deal Disasters

When you do it right, secondhand shopping is one of the most underrated money moves. Some stuff is practically built to be bought used, while other things should absolutely be bought new, no exceptions.

This section will teach you when to say "heck yes" to thrift finds and when to walk away fast. Done right, secondhand can feel like upgrading your life for pocket change.

- **Hack #56: Big Savings on Big Items**

Furniture, tech, gym equipment — buying these secondhand often saves hundreds without losing much quality.

- **Hack #57: Pre-Loved Designer Deals**

Love designer brands but hate the price tag? Pre-loved markets are packed with barely-used gems.

- **Hack #58: New Only for Safety Gear**

Things that protect your life (helmets, car seats) are non-negotiable. Always buy new.

- **Hack #59: Bookworm's Dream**

Used bookstores and online swaps let you read like royalty for the price of a cup of coffee.

- **Hack #60: Vintage Goldmine**

Unique vintage clothes, furniture, and decor are waiting in thrift stores if you're willing to dig.

The Cost-Per-Use Rule You Need – Math That Saves You

It's easy to get sticker shock when you see a high price tag. But cost-per-use math flips the script: the more you use something, the cheaper it actually becomes.

This section will show you how to spot when a "splurge" is a smart investment — and when it's just expensive clutter you don't need.

- **Hack #61: Cost-Per-Use Rule**

Take the price and divide it by the number of times you'll realistically use it. A $200 coat worn 200 times is cheaper per wear than a $20 shirt worn twice.

- **Hack #62: Invest in Daily Staples**

Shoes, bags, coats, jeans — the things you reach for daily are worth spending more on if they last longer.

- **Hack #63: Rent for Rarely-Used Stuff**

For things you'll only use once or twice a year (like a tuxedo or a power drill), renting saves money and storage space.

- **Hack #64: Ignore Flashy Price Tags**

Don't get hypnotized by markdowns or big sale signs. Cost-per-use matters way more than discounts.

- **Hack #65: Would I Use This Ten Times? Test**

If you can't picture yourself using it at least ten times, it's probably not worth buying.

Cashback Apps and Hacks – Free Money Without Lifting a Finger

Cashback isn't just for extreme couponers — it's for anyone who likes free money for things they already planned to buy. Used wisely, cashback apps and programs add up without making you do any extra work.

This section will walk you through the easiest ways to set up cashback systems that quietly build your savings every time you shop.

- **Hack #66: Cashback Extensions**

Install tools like Rakuten, Honey, or your favorite browser extension. They work behind the scenes to snag cashback on purchases you were making anyway.

- **Hack #67: Credit Card Cashback Strategy**

Use a credit card with cashback perks — but only if you pay it off in full every month. Debt interest will wipe out your wins fast.

- **Hack #68: Stack Cashback + Promo Codes**

Use cashback sites and promo codes together for maximum discounts. It's like giving your wallet a double high-five.

- **Hack #69: Gift Card Hacks**

Buy discounted gift cards for stores you already shop at—instant built-in savings with no extra effort.

- **Hack #70: Bank Cashback Programs**

Many banks offer cashback rewards if you activate their bonus offers — it takes two taps and can add up over time.

How to Stack Discounts Like a Ninja – Double Up, Win Big

One discount is great, but stacking multiple discounts is a life hack worthy of a standing ovation. Smart stackers know how to layer sales, promo codes, cashback, and loyalty points for epic wins.

This section will show you how to become a stacking master without feeling like you need a PhD in coupon science.

- **Hack #71: Double Sale Days**

Shop clearance sections during major holiday sales or special event days for extra-lowered prices.

- **Hack #72: Promo Code Hunt**

Before you check out online, spend two minutes searching for promo codes. It's basically free money waiting to be claimed.

- **Hack #73: Activate Cashback Last**

Always apply your discounts first, then click through the cashback portal — not the other way around — to lock in all the savings.

- **Hack #74: Combine Loyalty Points + Promo Codes**

Use your loyalty rewards *and* promo codes on the same purchase whenever possible for maximum effect.

- **Hack #75: Cart Abandonment Trick (Part 2)**

Leave your shopping cart sitting overnight. Brands will often send you a better deal just to get you to complete the checkout.

Master the Art of "Shopping Your Home" – Find Treasures You Forgot

Before you spend a dime on anything new, check what you already own. Odds are, you have forgotten treasures hiding in your closet, pantry, or junk drawer.

This section will show you how to "shop your home" first and turn what you already own into new, exciting finds — for free.

- **Hack #76: Closet Rediscovery Mission**

Go through your closet and challenge yourself to create new outfits with pieces you already have. It feels like free shopping.

- **Hack #77: Pantry Challenge**

Invent meals using only what's already in your fridge and pantry. It clears out food clutter and saves serious grocery money.

- **Hack #78: DIY Home Decor Refresh**

Rearranging your furniture or pulling forgotten decor items out of storage can completely refresh your space — no shopping required.

- **Hack #79: Repurpose Old Gadgets**

Old tech can become security cams, media players, or toys for kids. Give your old stuff a second life before tossing it.

- **Hack #80: Forgotten Gift Cards Hunt**

Search old wallets, drawers, and bags for forgotten gift cards. Hidden money hits differently.

Free Trials Without Regret – Try Everything, Pay for Nothing

Free trials are amazing — until you forget to cancel and get whacked with a big charge. The trick is using free trials with intention so you get all the perks and none of the pain.

This section teaches you how to try everything you want — and still keep your money safely where it belongs.

- **Hack #81: Set Instant Calendar Reminders**

When you start a free trial, set a reminder for two days before it ends. Future you will be grateful.

- **Hack #82: Use a Burner Email**

Sign up for free trials with a separate email account to avoid spam flooding your main inbox.

- **Hack #83: Trial Binge Days**

Use your free trial period to binge-watch shows, read magazines, or use premium features guilt-free — then cancel before paying.

- **Hack #84: Cancel Immediately (Still Keep the Trial)**

Some services let you cancel right after signing up, but still give you the full trial period. Less stress, full access.

- **Hack #85: Track Trials in Notes App**

Keep a running list of all your free trials with start and end dates. Staying organized keeps your wallet intact.

Managing Debt Without Losing Your Mind

Practical tricks to shrink your debt mountain without drowning in guilt or spreadsheets.

Debt can feel like that one party guest who never leaves — quietly sucking up all the snacks, air, and joy. But living with debt doesn't have to mean living under constant stress. It's not a moral failing or a life sentence — it's just a problem that needs a smarter plan.

This chapter is your shortcut map out of the chaos. You'll find doable ways to tackle debt, protect your sanity, and build momentum even if you're starting from behind. Guilt is banned. Complicated spreadsheets are optional. Progress is guaranteed.

Snowball vs. Avalanche – Picking the Right Fight

If you've ever Googled "how to pay off debt," you've probably seen two big strategies: the Snowball and the Avalanche. Both work, but depending on your brain wiring, one might work a lot better for you.

This section will help you pick the payoff style that keeps you motivated without feeling like you're climbing Everest. Momentum beats math sometimes, and you get to decide what makes you want to keep going.

- **Hack #86: Snowball Method**

Pay off your smallest debts first. Every quick win gives you a psychological boost that keeps you moving forward.

- **Hack #87: Avalanche Method**

Focus on debts with the highest interest rates first. It saves you more money overall, even if the victories take longer to show up.

- **Hack #88: Hybrid Hustle**

Combine both: start with one small win, then switch to the highest-interest debts—best of both worlds.

- **Hack #89: Visual Victory Tracker**

Create a visual tracker — like a chart or wall thermometer — to see your debts shrinking in real time.

- **Hack #90: Celebrate Tiny Wins**

Every time you wipe out a debt, even a tiny one, celebrate like you just paid off a mansion. Momentum matters.

The Micropayment Power Move – Crush Debt in Bite-Sized Chunks

Big debt feels heavy because we only think in big numbers. Micropayments flip the script by letting you chip away at balances every few days, without even feeling it.

This section will show you how breaking debt into tiny attacks can speed up your payoff timeline without squeezing your daily life.

- **Hack #91: Every Little Extra Counts**

Even $5 or $10 thrown at your balance between regular payments makes a bigger difference than you think.

- **Hack #92: Set Up Weekly Micro-Attacks**

Instead of one big payment a month, send small payments weekly. It keeps interest from stacking up.

- **Hack #93: Round-Up Trick**

Round your purchases up to the nearest $10 or $20 and throw the extra at your debt: invisible effort, real results.

- **Hack #94: Autopilot Micropayments**

Set small automatic transfers to your debts every week. It turns payoff into a background habit.

- **Hack #95: Spare Change Blitz**

Dump your spare change or cash-back bonuses straight into debt payments. Every little attack weakens the beast.

Credit Score Boosters You Can Start Today – Win the Game Faster

A better credit score means cheaper loans, better deals, and sometimes even easier job applications. Thankfully, you don't have to wait years to start climbing.

This section is packed with fast, practical wins to make your credit score work harder for you starting right now.

- **Hack #96: On-Time Payment Streak**

The easiest way to boost your score: never miss a payment, even if it's just the minimum.

- **Hack #97: Debt-to-Credit Ratio Hack**

Keep your credit usage under 30% of your limit. It shows lenders you're responsible (even if you're faking it a little).

- **Hack #98: Credit Limit Request Move**

Ask for a higher credit limit — but don't use it. A bigger gap between usage and limit = instant score boost.

- **Hack #99: Small Charges + Auto-Pay**

Put one small bill (like Netflix) on a credit card and auto-pay it off monthly to build a positive history effortlessly.

- **Hack #100: Credit Report Checkup**

Pull your free credit report and check for errors. Fixing mistakes could give your score a fast, easy lift.

The Fastest Way to Pay Off a Credit Card – Shortcuts That Work

Credit card debt is like a bad ex — charming at first, expensive forever. If you're tired of seeing half your payment eaten by interest, it's time to get strategic.

This section will teach you simple but aggressive moves to wipe out credit card debt faster, without living off ramen.

- **Hack #101: Highest Interest Attack**

Pay extra toward your highest-interest card first, while keeping minimums on the others. It's like stopping the worst bleeding first.

- **Hack #102: Balance Transfer Boost**

Transfer your balance to a 0% promo card if you can (and actually read the fine print).

- **Hack #103: Fixed Payment Plan**

Set a fixed payment way above the minimum and pretend the minimum doesn't exist. It speeds up the finish line.

- **Hack #104: Pay More Than Once a Month**

Splitting your payments into two or more a month reduces your average balance and interest charges.

- **Hack #105: Stop Using It Rule**

Once you start serious repayment, stop adding new charges. Otherwise, it's like bailing water from a sinking boat with a spoon.

How to Handle Student Loans (Without Crying) – Survive and Conquer

Student loans can feel endless, like a treadmill with no "off" button. But surviving (and even thriving) with them is possible if you play smart.

This section will help you keep your sanity, stay strategic, and still live your life while you pay them down.

- **Hack #106: Know Your Loan Types**

Federal? Private? Subsidized? Knowing the differences can open doors to better repayment options.

- **Hack #107: Income-Driven Plans**

If your loans are federal, you might qualify for lower payments based on your income — a breathing room lifesaver.

- **Hack #108: Employer Repayment Programs**

Some employers offer help paying student loans. Ask HR — free money is free money.

- **Hack #109: Extra Payments on Principal**

When you send extra money, ensure it goes toward principal, not just future interest.

- **Hack #110: Public Service Loan Forgiveness**

If you work in government, education, or non-profits, you might qualify for forgiveness after 10 years. Worth checking.

When to Consolidate (and When to Run) – Don't Get Trapped

Debt consolidation can be magic — or it can be a trap dressed up in shiny marketing. The difference is all in the details.

This section breaks down when consolidation helps... and when it just ties you up in new (and sometimes worse) chains.

- **Hack #111: Good Reason: Lower Interest Rates**

Consolidating at a lower rate makes sense if it saves you money in the long term.

- **Hack #112: Bad Reason: Bigger Payments**

If consolidation raises your monthly payment and you're already stretched thin, it's a red flag.

- **Hack #113: Loan Terms Check**

Watch out for sneaky extensions that lower your payment but massively increase your total interest paid.

- **Hack #114: One Monthly Payment Win**

Simplifying five debts into one payment can make budgeting easier and less stressful.

- **Hack #115: Stay Away If It Smells Like a Scam**

If a company promises "instant debt erasure" or "government forgiveness," run. Fast.

Mental Health and Debt – The Invisible Link

Debt isn't just numbers on a screen. It's a heavy, invisible weight on your brain, and ignoring that connection makes things harder.

This section will help you recognize the emotional toll and build mental muscles that make paying off debt (and feeling okay about it) way easier.

- **Hack #116: Debt Guilt Detox**

You are not your debt. Your self-worth isn't tied to your bank balance.

- **Hack #117: Focus on Progress, Not Perfection**

Tiny wins matter. Celebrate moving forward, even if it's slower than you want.

- **Hack #118: Debt-Free Daydreams**

Picture what life without debt will feel like. Hope is a powerful motivator.

- **Hack #119: Support Squad Creation**

Share your journey with a trusted friend or online community. Debt feels smaller when it's not a secret.

- **Hack #120: Mental Health Days Are Allowed**

Take breaks when you need them. Burnout doesn't help your wallet or your brain.

Protecting Your Wins Once You Pay It Off – Staying Free

Paying off a debt feels incredible, but keeping yourself out of the trap is the next battle.

This section gives you tools to protect your hard-won freedom and stay on offense, not defense.

- **Hack #121: Emergency Fund First**

Build an emergency stash before you start celebrating. Otherwise, the next surprise bill will drag you right back.

- **Hack #122: Cash Buffer Rule**

Keep a cushion between you and the credit card — even a few hundred bucks of buffer changes everything.

- **Hack #123: Spending Plan Upgrade**

Update your budget to reflect your new, debt-free life. Celebrate responsibly.

- **Hack #124: Accountability Partner**

Keep a trusted buddy who'll gently call you out if you start drifting back toward bad habits.

- **Hack #125: Debt-Free Identity Shift**

Think of yourself as someone who *doesn't live in debt* anymore. Identity shapes behavior.

How to Negotiate Lower Interest Rates – Conversations That Save You Thousands

Sometimes, a five-minute phone call can save you hundreds or thousands of dollars in interest. You just have to ask (nicely and persistently).

This section teaches you how to negotiate like a boss, without needing a finance degree or a magic wand.

- **Hack #126: Call and Ask**

Seriously. Just call your credit card company and ask for a lower interest rate. The worst they can say is no.

- **Hack #127: Mention Good Payment History**

If you've been a loyal, on-time customer, bring it up. Companies hate losing good customers.

- **Hack #128: Shop Around for Leverage**

Let them know you've found better offers elsewhere. A little competition lights a fire under them.

- **Hack #129: Stay Polite but Firm**

Kindness opens doors. Confidence keeps them open.

- **Hack #130: If They Say No, Try Again Later**

Sometimes it's about catching the right agent on the right day. Persistence pays.

Building Momentum When You Feel Stuck – Speeding Up When It Feels Slow

Sometimes paying off debt feels like you're running through molasses — slow, frustrating, never-ending. That's normal. And it's beatable.

This section gives you tricks to turbocharge your motivation and snap yourself out of the sticky middle.

- **Hack #131: Micro-Milestone Celebrations**

Every $100, $500, and $1000 paid off deserves a mini victory dance.

- **Hack #132: Debt Countdown Visuals**

Create countdown trackers you can color in. Watching progress is addictively motivating.

- **Hack #133: Side Hustle Sprints**

Short bursts of extra income — babysitting, selling stuff, tutoring — can fund big leaps forward.

- **Hack #134: Gamify It**

Turn debt payoff into a game: challenges, rewards, points. Trick your brain into chasing wins.

- **Hack #135: Remember Your Why**

Keep a note somewhere visible about why you're doing this. Freedom beats frustration every time.

The Money Mindset Shift

Change your money story from "I'm bad at this" to "I'm playing to win."

If you've ever thought, "I'm just not good with money," you're not alone — and you're not doomed, either. Most of us were never taught how to handle money in ways that feel good, practical, and human. But here's the secret: being "good with money" isn't a talent you're born with. It's a skill you build, like learning to drive or bake a cake without setting off the smoke alarm.

This chapter isn't about budgeting harder or earning six figures overnight. It's about flipping your internal script so that managing money feels less like a punishment... and more like a game you can win.

Why Budgeting Isn't Punishment – It's Power

Somewhere along the way, budgeting got a bad reputation — like it's a joyless spreadsheet telling you "no" all day. But a real budget isn't there to scold you. It's there to *free you* from stress, guesswork, and panic spending.

When you treat a budget like a map to the life you actually want (instead of a cage you have to live inside), everything shifts. In this section, you'll learn how budgeting can feel like choosing your own adventure, not serving a sentence.

- **Hack #136: Permission to Spend Plan**

Think of your budget as allowing you to spend guilt-free on the stuff you love.

- **Hack #137: Fun Fund Category**

Always build "fun money" into your budget. If there's no joy allowed, your budget will self-destruct faster than a bad New Year's resolution.

- **Hack #138: Monthly Check-In Ritual**

Set a chill date with yourself to check your numbers. Make it cozy: coffee, music, snacks — not spreadsheets in a panic.

- **Hack #139: Budget Like a Playlist**

Mix essentials (bills) with hits (fun stuff) and future jams (savings goals). Good playlists — and budgets — balance it all.

- **Hack #140: Celebrate Zero-Based Budgeting**

When every dollar has a job, you stop wondering where your money disappeared. Hint: it's not punishment. It's clarity.

"Freedom Over Stuff" Mentality – Choosing Better Wins

If you chase stuff forever, your wallet will never be safe. But if you chase freedom — free time, choices, peace — money suddenly becomes your ally instead of your leash.

This section will help you train your brain to crave *freedom wins* more than shopping hits. Spoiler: freedom feels better (and lasts longer) than anything you can cart out of a mall.

- **Hack #141: Crave Time, Not Things**

Shift your goals from "buy more" to "live more." Time and freedom are the ultimate flex.

- **Hack #142: Experience Wishlist**

Make a list of experiences you want — trips, workshops, days off — instead of just stuff you want to own.

- **Hack #143: Exit the Upgrade Trap**

You don't need a newer phone, bigger house, or flashier car every two years. Real upgrades are invisible — like peace of mind.

- **Hack #144: Freedom as a Status Symbol**

Normalize celebrating paid-off debt, free weekends, and low-stress living as the new "luxury lifestyle."

- **Hack #145: Money Buys Options**

Focus on using money to buy options (quit jobs, move cities, start side gigs), not just more clutter.

Gamifying Your Financial Goals – Play Your Way to Success

Let's be honest: "serious adulting" sounds exhausting. Gamifying your goals — turning them into small, winnable challenges — makes saving and managing money way more fun.

In this section, you'll learn how to trick your brain into chasing wins like it's playing a game… and rack up real-life victories along the way.

- **Hack #146: Savings Challenge Cards**

Make a stack of $5, $10, and $20 savings challenges you pull at random and complete like missions.

- **Hack #147: Debt Payoff Bingo**

Create a bingo board for milestones like "Paid off $100" or "Skipped takeout and saved $25." Reward yourself for every bingo.

- **Hack #148: Boss Battle Bonuses**

Big wins (like paying off a card or hitting a savings goal) deserve special celebrations. Treat yourself like you beat the final level.

- **Hack #149: Level-Up Your Auto-Savings**

Every time you complete a savings month, raise your auto-transfer by $5. Tiny level-ups = massive results.

- **Hack #150: Scoreboards and Trackers**

Track your progress visually. Watching your savings or debt payoff graph grow feels like leveling up IRL.

Building Wealth With Small Wins – The Secret to Massive Growth

Forget giant leaps and lottery wins. Real wealth is built one small, repeatable win at a time. Consistency beats intensity every single day.

This section will show you how celebrating small money wins (and stacking them) creates unstoppable momentum — and a lot less stress.

- **Hack #151: The Compounding Tiny Win**

Saving $10 a week might sound boring… until you realize it's $500+ a year you didn't have before.

- **Hack #152: Habit Over Hype**

Getting rich slowly and steadily beats trying to hit financial home runs once in a while.

- **Hack #153: Automate and Chill**

Set up automatic savings and bill payments so you win by default — even on days you don't feel like being smart.

- **Hack #154: Momentum Beats Motivation**

Start small, keep going. Motivation is nice, but momentum keeps you winning when you're tired or distracted.

- **Hack #155: Progress Streaks**

Track how many weeks you've stuck to your plan. Breaking a good streak hurts more — so you'll want to keep going.

Stop Comparing Your Wallet to Instagram – Kill the Noise

Comparison is a thief — especially when you're comparing your real life to someone else's highlight reel. Spoiler alert: most people flexing luxury lives online are flexing debt, not wealth.

This section is all about tuning out the noise so you can build your money life based on what *you* actually want — not what looks good to strangers.

- **Hack #156: Mute the Flexers**

Unfollow or mute accounts that make you feel behind. Protect your energy and your wallet.

- **Hack #157: Reality Check Rituals**

Every time you catch yourself feeling "behind," write down three real wins you've had this month. (Paying rent counts.)

- **Hack #158: Financial Goals, Not Performances**

Your money life is a private game — not a performance for likes or followers.

- **Hack #159: Behind the Scenes Matters More**

The person quietly maxing their retirement account is winning harder than the one showing off a rented car.

- **Hack #160: Offline Wins Are Real Wins**

Building an emergency fund, getting out of debt, sleeping without money stress — that's flex-worthy.

Talking to Your Future Self (Literally) – The Best Pep Talk

Future You isn't some vague concept — it's a real person you're building right now. And Future You deserves better than chaos and panic attacks over car repairs.

This section will help you build a relationship with Future You, so you make decisions today that you'll be ridiculously grateful for tomorrow.

- **Hack #161: Write Letters to Future You**

Jot down notes about why you're saving, what dreams you have, and how good it'll feel when you hit those goals.

- **Hack #162: Visualize a Day in Future You's Life**

Picture waking up debt-free, stress-free, or financially independent. Make it vivid.

- **Hack #163: Micro-Yes Decisions**

Every tiny smart money move is a yes to Future You living a way cooler life.

- **Hack #164: Future You's Emergency Fund**

Don't save because you "should." Save because Future You will high-five you hard when the fridge dies.

- **Hack #165: Mini Time Machine Moments**

Before big money decisions, ask: "Will Future Me be pumped about this... or pissed?"

Celebrating Tiny Money Victories – Motivation on Tap

Tiny victories aren't "cute" — they're how you stay alive in the game long enough to win big. Every $50 saved or debt payment made is proof that you're moving in the right direction.

This section shows how turning small wins into tiny parties fuels big, long-term success without waiting for some mythical "someday."

- **Hack #166: Victory Jars**

Every time you hit a goal, throw a note or a dollar into a jar. Watch your wins stack up visually.

- **Hack #167: Snackable Rewards**

Celebrate each milestone (like saving your first $500) with a little treat — ice cream, a cheap coffee, a guilt-free Netflix night.

- **Hack #168: Stacking Tiny Wins**

Focus on building momentum. Every small success stacks up until suddenly, you've crossed a major finish line.

- **Hack #169: Mini-Milestone Trackers**

Use charts, graphs, or even sticker charts (yes, like a 5-year-old) to track progress visually.

- **Hack #170: Positive Spiral Trick**

Success breeds success. Celebrating small wins makes you want to create even more.

Using Affirmations Without Feeling Silly – Brain Tricks That Work

Affirmations can feel cheesy... but they work because your brain believes whatever it hears most often. Why not make sure it's hearing things that actually build you up?

This section shows you how to use affirmations in a way that feels natural, powerful, and actually useful — not cringe.

- **Hack #171: Money Mantra Morning**

Start your day with one simple phrase like, "I make smart, powerful choices with my money."

- **Hack #172: Proof-Based Affirmations**

Ground your affirmations in real action: "I saved $50 this week — I *am* someone who handles money well."

- **Hack #173: Sticky Note Strategy**

Write a few affirmations and stick them on your mirror, laptop, or fridge where you'll actually see them.

- **Hack #174: Affirmation Playlist**

Record yourself saying a few affirmations and listen back while driving or walking. (Hearing your own voice = extra powerful.)

- **Hack #175: Affirm It, Then Act It**

Pair affirmations with real moves. Saying "I'm building wealth" hits harder right after transferring money to savings.

Reframing "Sacrifice" as "Strategy" – Flip the Script

When you think of smart money moves as painful sacrifices, you'll resent them. When you frame them as power moves that future-proof your life, you'll feel unstoppable.

This section teaches you how to rebrand your smart decisions as winning strategies — not punishments.

- **Hack #176: Strategic Trade-Offs**

Skipping a new phone this year = funding a vacation next year. That's a win, not a sacrifice.

- **Hack #177: Long Game Language**

Tell yourself, "I'm choosing bigger wins," not "I'm giving something up."

- **Hack #178: Smart Budgeting = Freedom Building**

Every dollar you don't waste today buys more freedom for your future life.

- **Hack #179: Decision Affirmation Trick**

When making a tough choice, remind yourself: "This isn't forever. This is building something better."

- **Hack #180: Sacrifice Feels Different When It's Voluntary**

Choosing to delay gratification feels powerful. Being forced to delay it feels awful. Focus on the *choice*.

It's a Skillset, Not a Character Flaw – Anyone Can Learn This

You're not "bad with money" — you're just still learning, like everyone else. Managing money is a skill, like driving or baking: nobody is magically good at it on day one.

This section is your permission slip to drop the shame and treat money like any other skill you can totally get better at with practice.

- **Hack #181: Beginner's Mindset Magic**

You're allowed to not know everything yet. Stay curious, stay learning.

- **Hack #182: Money Skills Are Built, Not Born**

Even rich people once didn't know what they were doing. Everybody starts somewhere.

- **Hack #183: Progress Beats Perfection**

Getting 1% better with money every month still means massive change over time.

- **Hack #184: Failures Are Just Lessons**

A bad financial decision isn't a death sentence. It's a textbook.

- **Hack #185: You're Playing the Long Game**

You don't have to be perfect today. You just have to stay in the game.

Budgeting for People Who Hate Budgeting

Manage your money without feeling like you signed up for financial bootcamp.

Budgeting sounds about as fun as mandatory gym class — rules, restrictions, and zero snacks. No wonder so many people avoid it like it's a punishment. But real-life, human budgeting doesn't have to be miserable or complicated. You don't need spreadsheets that look like rocket launch plans or apps that send you passive-aggressive alerts.

This chapter is all about finding the budgeting style that fits *you* — the non-accountant, freedom-loving version of you who still wants their money to behave. Let's ditch the guilt and find a system that feels like a life upgrade, not a life sentence.

Reverse Budgeting – Save First, Chill Later

Instead of trying to track every dollar you spend, reverse budgeting flips the system: you save first, cover your essentials, and whatever's left is yours to enjoy guilt-free.

This section helps you build a money flow that feels automatic and low-stress — no spreadsheets or panic attacks required.

- **Hack #186: Auto-Save Strategy**

Schedule automatic transfers to savings and investments as soon as your paycheck hits.

- **Hack #187: Essentials Come First**

Handle your must-pay stuff — rent, groceries, utilities — before you even blink at the fun money.

- **Hack #188: Spend the Leftovers**

Whatever's left after saving and bills is yours to use however you want. No guilt, no second-guessing.

- **Hack #189: Prioritize Freedom Over Control**

Reverse budgeting gives you permission to enjoy your money without feeling reckless.

- **Hack #190: No Micromanaging Required**

This system works great for people who hate logging every coffee and snack into an app.

3-Category Budget – Keep It So Simple It's Foolproof

The more complicated your budget is, the faster it'll crash and burn. A three-category budget keeps it brutally simple: Essentials, Savings, Fun.

In this section, you'll learn how to break your money into three easy buckets that don't require a finance degree to understand.

- **Hack #191: Essentials Bucket**

Cover rent, utilities, groceries — the must-haves to stay alive and sane.

- **Hack #192: Savings Bucket**

Send money into your emergency fund, future goals, or investments immediately after essentials.

- **Hack #193: Fun Money Bucket**

Everything else — coffee dates, hobbies, late-night pizza — goes here.

- **Hack #194: Easy Percentage Rule**

Start with a rough 50/30/20 split (Essentials/Fun/Savings) and adjust to what feels realistic.

- **Hack #195: Visual Bucket Labels**

Color-code or label your buckets so you can instantly see where your money is flowing.

Weekly 10-Minute Check-Ins – Quick Wins, Big Impact

Forget long, painful budget meetings. You can stay on top of your money with a chill 10-minute check-in every week.

This section shows you how tiny weekly moments can keep you from spiraling into budget chaos.

- **Hack #196: Set a Standing Date**

Pick a consistent time (Sunday morning? Friday night?) to peek at your accounts without judgment.

- **Hack #197: Only Look for Leaks**

You're not building spreadsheets — you're just spotting obvious leaks ("Oops, six takeout meals again").

- **Hack #198: Mini Tweaks Matter**

Tiny course corrections each week save you from massive disasters later.

- **Hack #199: Celebrate the Good Stuff**

Notice and celebrate every little thing you did right, even if it's small.

- **Hack #200: No Punishment Zone**

Checking your budget should feel like a pit stop, not a performance review.

Visual Budgets – Make Your Money Make Sense

Numbers on a screen can feel meaningless. Visual budgets turn your money into pictures, colors, and graphs your brain can actually enjoy looking at.

This section will help you create a budget you can *see* winning.

- **Hack #201: Color Code Everything**

Assign colors to spending categories so you can tell at a glance where your cash goes.

- **Hack #202: Progress Thermometers**

Draw savings or debt payoff trackers you can color in every time you hit a milestone.

- **Hack #203: Budget Pie Charts**

Split your spending into colorful slices. Big splurges stand out instantly.

- **Hack #204: Savings Graphs**

Watching a graph grow is ridiculously satisfying — and addictive in the best way.

- **Hack #205: Wall Charts or Apps**

Use whatever visual system fits your vibe — fancy apps or just sticky notes on the fridge.

Budgeting with Irregular Income – Taming the Rollercoaster

If your income swings wildly (freelancers, gig workers, commission earners — I see you), traditional monthly budgets won't cut it.

This section teaches you how to budget when payday feels more like a lottery than a paycheck.

- **Hack #206: Base Budget Off Your Worst Month**

Plan your budget based on your lowest expected income. Surprises become bonuses, not disasters.

- **Hack #207: Priority Pay Order**

List bills and essentials from most important to least and pay them in that order as money arrives.

- **Hack #208: Seasonal Squirreling**

In good months, hoard extra cash to cover the lean ones.

- **Hack #209: Separate Business and Personal Money**

If you're self-employed, keep business and personal accounts separate to avoid mixing chaos with chaos.

- **Hack #210: Emergency Fund First Rule**

Before you upgrade anything, build a two-month living expenses fund. It's pure peace of mind.

Zero-Based Budgeting – Giving Every Dollar a Job

Zero-based budgeting doesn't mean you're broke — it means every dollar is assigned somewhere before the month starts.

This section shows how giving every dollar a mission makes your money behave better — and helps you sleep at night.

- **Hack #211: Name Every Dollar**

Before you spend, assign each dollar to a bill, savings, fun, or future goal.

- **Hack #212: Fill the Gaps First**

Prioritize needs before wants — it's way easier to enjoy spending when you're not dodging late fees.

- **Hack #213: Adjust Monthly**

Your life changes every month — so should your zero-based plan.

- **Hack #214: Fake Deadlines Trick**

Pretend bills are due a week early. You'll never panic over real due dates again.

- **Hack #215: No Free Agents**

If a dollar doesn't have a job, it will wander off to nonsense purchases. Give it a home.

Budgeting for Couples – Money Talks Without the Fighting

Talking about money with someone else can turn into an Olympic-level argument if you're not careful. But it doesn't have to.

This section shows how to team up on budgeting without throwing salad bowls across the kitchen.

- **Hack #216: Weekly Money Dates**

Schedule short, chill money talks over coffee or wine — not during fights.

- **Hack #217: Separate Fun Funds**

Give each partner their own no-questions-asked fun money.

- **Hack #218: Big Goals First**

Agree on major savings goals together before arguing about daily spending habits.

- **Hack #219: Transparency Wins**

Share logins or overviews so no one feels left out (or left guessing).

- **Hack #220: Compromise Budgets**

Blend your styles — one saver + one spender = balanced budget dreams.

Budgeting Without Guilt – Forgiveness Over Perfection

Perfection is the enemy of a real, livable budget. You'll overspend sometimes. You'll miss a savings target. It's fine. You're not a robot.

This section teaches you how to budget with forgiveness — and keep moving forward without spiraling into shame.

- **Hack #221: Build in Mistake Space**

Expect a few oops moments. Budget a little slack for "life happens" money.

- **Hack #222: Zero-Guilt Resets**

Blew your budget last month? Cool. Reset and start fresh. No punishments required.

- **Hack #223: Focus on Net Progress**

One bad week doesn't erase months of wins. Zoom out and look at the bigger trend.

- **Hack #224: Self-Talk Check**

Catch yourself if you start saying, "I'm bad with money." Switch to, "I'm getting better every month."

- **Hack #225: Guilt-Free Splurges**

Allow occasional splurges on purpose. Planned fun keeps you from feeling trapped.

The Anti-Budget – For the Truly Budget Allergic

If you can't stand traditional budgets at all, welcome to the Anti-Budget. It's budgeting for people who hate budgeting so much they refuse to say the word.

This section shows you how to control your money without ever using spreadsheets, categories, or apps.

- **Hack #226: Skim Savings Off the Top**

Set an automatic percentage of every paycheck to savings first. Then forget about it.

- **Hack #227: Pay Essentials, Ignore the Rest**

Once bills are paid, live on what's left. No tracking daily spending unless you want to.

- **Hack #228: Cash-Only Trick**

Withdraw a set amount of spending money in cash. When it's gone, you're done.

- **Hack #229: Monthly Reset Rule**

Every month, check if savings + essentials happened. If yes, success. If not, tweak.

- **Hack #230: Freedom First Focus**

The Anti-Budget is about buying back freedom — not counting every coffee.

Finding Hidden Money in Your Life

Uncover cash hiding in your couch cushions, subscriptions, and habits.

You don't always need a raise to boost your bank account — sometimes, you just need a flashlight and a little curiosity. Money leaks, forgotten treasures, and lazy subscriptions are secretly draining your wallet while you're busy living life.

This chapter is your treasure map to the cash you already have. No extreme couponing. No selling a kidney. Just sneaky, smart moves to grab the money that's been hiding right under your nose.

Selling Forgotten Items – Turning Clutter Into Cash

Your house is basically a mini goldmine of stuff you forgot you even owned. That random exercise bike, those jeans that never fit, the gadgets gathering dust — they're cash in disguise.

This section helps you turn your forgotten clutter into real money without feeling like you're staging a full garage sale extravaganza.

- **Hack #231: One Closet at a Time**

Tackle one closet, drawer, or room at a time. Bite-sized missions beat overwhelming marathons.

- **Hack #232: The "Would I Buy This Today?" Test**

If you wouldn't spend real money on it today, it's time to let it go (and sell it).

- **Hack #233: Snap, Post, Repeat**

Take five quick photos, post them online, and move on. Don't overthink it — messy pics sell too.

- **Hack #234: Batch for Bigger Platforms**

Group similar stuff together and post bundles — books, baby clothes, kitchen gadgets.

- **Hack #235: Cash Before Nostalgia**

If it's not a treasured heirloom, prioritize the money over the memories.

Canceling Sneaky Subscriptions – Slay the $9.99 Monsters

Subscriptions are like tiny vampires — they bleed you slowly until you barely notice the bite. One forgotten app or magazine turns into hundreds lost every year.

This section shows you how to hunt them down, cancel ruthlessly, and keep your wallet happily unbitten.

- **Hack #236: Subscription Scavenger Hunt**

Go through your bank and PayPal history for the last three months. Bet you find some surprises.

- **Hack #237: The Double-Price Test**

Would you still pay if the price doubled tomorrow? If not, cancel.

- **Hack #238: Cancel First, Re-Subscribe Later**

You can always re-subscribe later if you miss it. Fear of missing out is expensive.

- **Hack #239: Rotation Method**

Rotate services seasonally — Disney+ one month, Hulu the next. Keeps things fresh and cheaper.

- **Hack #240: Hidden App Subscriptions**

Check your phone settings (Apple ID or Google Play) — tons of sneaky subscriptions hide there.

Gift Card Treasure Hunts – Free Money You Forgot

Gift cards are free money — but only if you remember to use them. Too often, they gather dust or expire before they ever hit your wallet.

This section will help you dig up old cards, cash them in, and turn them into instant spending power.

- **Hack #241: Old Wallets and Purses Raid**

Search through every old wallet, bag, and jacket pocket. Treasure often hides there.

- **Hack #242: Email Inbox Excavation**

Use search terms like "gift card" or "voucher" — sometimes digital cards hide in your email.

- **Hack #243: Partial Card Trick**

Even if there's only $1.53 left on a card, use it. Small balances still count as free money.

- **Hack #244: Regift (Strategically)**

If you'll never use a card, regift it thoughtfully — it's better than letting it rot.

- **Hack #245: Exchange or Sell Unwanted Cards**

Use online platforms to trade or sell cards you won't use for ones you actually will.

Bank Statement Scavenger Hunt – Find Leaks You Forgot

Bank statements are basically secret confessionals. Hidden fees, double charges, sneaky subscriptions — it's all there, waiting to be found.

This section shows you how a quick scan through your accounts can reclaim cash you didn't even know you lost.

- **Hack #246: Highlight the Weird Stuff**

Every charge you don't recognize or forgot about? Highlight it and investigate.

- **Hack #247: Fee Refund Phone Calls**

Call your bank or card company about weird fees. Often, they'll refund them if you ask nicely.

- **Hack #248: Duplicate Subscriptions Check**

Sometimes you accidentally pay for the same service twice. Cancel one, bask in the savings.

- **Hack #249: Annual Charges Sneak Attack**

Annual charges hide better than monthly ones. Check for once-a-year leaks you forgot existed.

- **Hack #250: Request Refunds on Mistakes**

If you find errors or double billing, ask for a refund immediately. Companies are usually too lazy to argue.

Tiny Negotiations, Big Wins – Saving Money With a Few Brave Questions

You don't have to scream, threaten, or cry to get a better deal. Sometimes, just politely asking can put real money back in your pocket.

This section teaches you how to negotiate tiny costs down — and why a few brave conversations can save you hundreds a year.

- **Hack #251: Bill Discount Dance**

Call your internet, phone, or insurance company and ask for a loyalty discount or promotional rate.

- **Hack #252: Script It, Say It**

Prepare a simple script like, "Is there a better rate available for loyal customers?" and stick to it.

- **Hack #253: Credit Card Rate Requests**

Call your card company and ask for a lower interest rate. Worst case, they say no. Best case, you save a ton.

- **Hack #254: Medical Bill Magic**

Always ask if there's a cash discount, payment plan, or financial aid option before paying a medical bill.

- **Hack #255: Bundle and Save**

Ask if bundling services (insurance, streaming, anything) can get you a better price.

Unused Perks and Benefits – Hidden Gold Mines

You're probably sitting on perks you forgot you had — freebies, reimbursements, and hidden benefits buried in your memberships.

This section helps you uncover the bonuses you're already entitled to — and put them to work.

- **Hack #256: Credit Card Perk Check**

Many cards offer travel insurance, purchase protection, or discounts you're not even using.

- **Hack #257: Employer Reimbursements**

Check if your job reimburses education, fitness, transport, or work-from-home costs.

- **Hack #258: Membership Freebies**

Gyms, clubs, and even loyalty programs often offer free guest passes, classes, or goodies.

- **Hack #259: App Discounts and Bonuses**

Dig into your apps — delivery services, rideshares, and banks often hide discount offers in small print.

- **Hack #260: Healthcare Perks**

Some health insurance plans cover gym memberships, mental health apps, or nutrition counseling. Check your benefits.

Utility Company Hidden Discounts – Saving on Life's Boring Bills

Utility bills feel like a fixed, boring part of life — but often, they're quietly negotiable or packed with hidden discounts.

This section shows you how to tame your power, water, and internet bills without sacrificing comfort.

- **Hack #261: Budget Billing Plans**

Ask your utility company if they offer a budget billing plan to flatten seasonal bill spikes.

- **Hack #262: Low-Income Discount Programs**

Some companies offer discounts based on income levels — but you usually have to ask.

- **Hack #263: Efficiency Rebates**

Switching to energy-efficient appliances often earns rebates. Check your local energy provider's site.

- **Hack #264: Loyalty Rate Inquiries**

Call and ask if long-time customers qualify for loyalty discounts or better plans.

- **Hack #265: Usage Reviews**

Some companies offer free usage audits to help you lower your bills without changing your lifestyle.

Old Accounts and Forgotten Money – Claim What's Yours

Believe it or not, you might have actual unclaimed money floating out there — forgotten bank accounts, refund checks, or insurance payouts.

This section gives you the tools to find money you already earned but never collected.

- **Hack #266: Unclaimed Property Websites**

Search your name at your country's unclaimed property registry — you might find forgotten checks or refunds.

- **Hack #267: Old Banks and Credit Unions**

If you ever opened an account and forgot about it, there could be a dormant balance waiting.

- **Hack #268: Class Action Lawsuit Claims**

You might qualify for settlements from lawsuits without even knowing it — search for open claims.

- **Hack #269: Utility Deposits**

Old electric or internet companies sometimes owe deposit refunds after you move or cancel.

- **Hack #270: Pension or Retirement Funds**

Worked somewhere briefly years ago? You might still have a small pension or 401(k) floating out there.

Investing Without Fear (Or FOMO)

A simple, no-jargon guide to making your money grow while you sleep.

Investing sounds like something reserved for rich people in suits—or sweaty day traders glued to ten monitors. But the truth is, investing isn't about gambling, getting rich overnight, or being smarter than everyone else. It's about playing the long game, planting seeds today that turn into serious freedom later.

This chapter is your no-scary-stuff, no-jargon introduction to investing. You don't need to be a financial wizard to start. You just need a few simple moves, some patience, and the ability to mute the next guy yelling about Bitcoin on TikTok.

Starting Small: The $10 Investment – Tiny Moves, Huge Impact

Most people don't invest because they think they need thousands of dollars to even get started. Good news: you don't. Ten bucks is enough.

This section shows how even tiny investments can build momentum—and why starting is way more important than starting big.

- **Hack #271: Micro-Investing Apps**

Apps like Acorns and Robinhood let you invest small amounts. No suits required.

- **Hack #272: Buy Fractional Shares**

Many platforms let you buy slices of stocks or ETFs, not just whole ones. $10 can own you a piece of Amazon.

- **Hack #273: Set a Weekly Micro-Auto-Invest**

Set an automatic $5 or $10 investment every week. Tiny, painless, but powerful over time.

- **Hack #274: Celebrate First Investments**

Even investing $1 makes you an investor. Own it. Brag about it. Celebrate it.

- **Hack #275: Momentum Over Magnitude**

Small, consistent actions always beat giant plans that never happen.

What Is an Index Fund? – The Lazy Genius's Best Friend

An index fund is the ultimate "set it and forget it" tool—and no, it's not complicated. It's just a basket of stocks that follows the market automatically.

This section shows why index funds are basically cheat codes for building wealth without learning to speak fluent Wall Street.

- **Hack #276: One Fund = Hundreds of Stocks**

An index fund gives you tiny pieces of hundreds of companies at once. Instant diversification.

- **Hack #277: Low Fees = More Money for You**

Index funds usually have super-low fees because there's no fancy manager pretending they're smarter than the market.

- **Hack #278: Market Matching > Market Timing**

Instead of trying to beat the market, you ride it. Long-term, this wins almost every time.

- **Hack #279: Vanguard, Fidelity, Schwab Basics**

Major providers like Vanguard and Fidelity offer rock-solid index funds. No fancy stuff needed.

- **Hack #280: Time is the Real Magic**

The longer your money stays invested, the more it snowballs—without needing any extra brainpower from you.

Robo-Advisors for Busy Brains – Smart Investing on Autopilot

If the idea of picking investments gives you hives, robo-advisors are your dream team. They automate everything based on your goals and risk tolerance.

This section shows how busy, non-expert humans can still crush investing with basically zero extra brain energy.

- **Hack #281: Set It and Forget It Setup**

You answer a few questions about goals and comfort with risk. The robo does the rest.

- **Hack #282: Automatic Rebalancing**

Robo-advisors adjust your portfolio automatically over time, keeping it balanced without you lifting a finger.

- **Hack #283: Low Minimums**

Many robo-advisors let you start with as little as $5 or $10.

- **Hack #284: Flat Fees, No Fancy Sales Pitches**

You pay a tiny management fee, but it's clear, upfront, and usually cheaper than hiring a human advisor.

- **Hack #285: Emotion-Proof Your Investing**

Because a robot is managing it, you won't panic sell the next time the market sneezes.

The "Invest and Forget It" Strategy – Let Time Do the Heavy Lifting

Investing works best when you treat it like a slow cooker, not a microwave. Start the process, walk away, come back later to delicious results.

This section shows why tinkering less often makes you richer—and keeps your blood pressure down.

- **Hack #286: Auto-Invest Monthly**

Set up monthly auto-contributions and never think about them again. Smooth and steady wins.

- **Hack #287: Don't Chase Headlines**

Market booms and crashes make news. Ignore it. Your plan doesn't change.

- **Hack #288: Resist the Tweak Temptation**

Changing strategies constantly costs you more than riding through ups and downs.

- **Hack #289: Check Once a Year, Not Every Day**

Review your investments yearly to adjust contributions or celebrate wins—not to panic.

- **Hack #290: Long-Term Mindset = Wealth**

Investing is about decades, not weeks. Stay calm, stay in the game, win big.

Avoiding Crypto and Meme Stock FOMO – Stay Smart, Stay Rich

It's tempting to chase whatever shiny thing is blowing up online — Bitcoin, meme stocks, NFTs, whatever's trending today. But chasing hype is the fastest way to get burned.

This section shows how to build real wealth without falling for internet-fueled get-rich-quick traps.

- **Hack #291: You're Not Late to Anything**

Real wealth is slow and boring. Missing the next Bitcoin boom isn't a tragedy.

- **Hack #292: Hype = Risk = Pain**

If everyone's screaming about it online, the smart money probably already left the party.

- **Hack #293: Speculation ≠ Investing**

Speculating is gambling. Investing is building. Know which one you're doing.

- **Hack #294: Play Money Rule**

If you must dabble in crypto or stocks for fun, use tiny amounts you're totally fine losing.

- **Hack #295: FOMO Filters**

Before jumping in, ask yourself: "Would I buy this if nobody else was talking about it?"

Understanding Risk Without Panic – Stay in the Game

Investing always involves risk — but it doesn't have to involve panic attacks. Learning how risk really works makes you a stronger, calmer investor.

This section helps you build your risk muscle without freaking yourself out.

- **Hack #296: Short-Term = Volatile, Long-Term = Stable**

Stocks jump around like toddlers short-term. Over decades, they smooth out and climb.

- **Hack #297: Risk Tolerance Self-Check**

Ask yourself: would I rather make a little less but sleep at night? Or stomach ups and downs for bigger rewards?

- **Hack #298: Diversify to Soften Blows**

Spread your money across lots of investments, not just one. Diversification = natural armor.

- **Hack #299: Know Your Investment Horizon**

Money you need in 2 years = savings account. Money you need in 20 years = invest it.

- **Hack #300: Expect (Not Fear) Drops**

Market drops are normal, expected, and temporary. Plan for them mentally ahead of time.

Compound Interest: The World's Best Magic Trick

Compound interest is so powerful it basically feels like financial wizardry. And the earlier you start, the stronger the magic gets.

This section explains why tiny investments grow into huge results without needing bigger paychecks or bigger sacrifices.

- **Hack #301: Interest on Interest = Snowball Effect**

Your money earns money... and then that money earns even more money. Infinite loop of awesome.

- **Hack #302: Early Start = Exponential Wins**

Starting even five years earlier doubles or triples your results later.

- **Hack #303: Time > Talent**

You don't have to pick the perfect stocks. Starting early and being consistent beats being brilliant.

- **Hack #304: Stay Invested Through Bumps**

Every day your money stays invested, the compound magic works harder for you.

- **Hack #305: Patience Pays in Millions**

People who stay invested over 20+ years often see results they never thought possible.

Retirement Accounts 101 – Free Money You Shouldn't Ignore

Retirement might feel light-years away, but investing in it now is one of the smartest (and easiest) wins available.

This section shows you how to build future freedom while barely noticing today.

- **Hack #306: Employer Match = Instant Raise**

If your company matches 401(k) contributions, it's free money. Max it out if you can.

- **Hack #307: Tax Break Heaven**

Money in retirement accounts often grows tax-free or tax-deferred. Translation: bigger piles later.

- **Hack #308: IRA Basics**

If your job doesn't offer a plan, open an IRA (Individual Retirement Account). Still tax perks, still freedom.

- **Hack #309: Auto-Increase Contributions**

Set your 401(k) or IRA to auto-increase 1% every year. You'll barely notice it now but love it later.

- **Hack #310: Don't Raid the Piggy Bank**

Borrowing from your retirement accounts feels tempting — but it can cost you thousands. Protect that money like it's your future (because it is).

Investing Even If You're Broke – Small Steps, Big Futures

Feeling broke doesn't mean you have to sit out the investing game. Even $5 a week starts building a financial future worth fighting for.

This section shows how to get in the game no matter what your starting line looks like.

- **Hack #311: Start Stupid Small**

$5, $10, whatever you can scrape together — just start. Size doesn't matter; consistency does.

- **Hack #312: Prioritize Over Perfect**

Focus on regular investing, not perfect timing. Perfect is a myth anyway.

- **Hack #313: Use Found Money**

Tax refunds, bonuses, birthday cash — put a slice into investments instead of just spending it.

- **Hack #314: Invest Your Raises**

Every time you get a raise, invest part of it before lifestyle creep eats it all.

- **Hack #315: Micro Wins Compound**

Tiny amounts don't feel powerful at first — but stacked over years, they turn into serious freedom.

Building Your Emergency Fund Without Stress

Set up your financial safety net without sacrificing your sanity—or your Friday night pizza.

Emergency funds are the financial equivalent of a superhero cape. They're not glamorous, but when life throws a car breakdown, medical bill, or unexpected job hiccup your way, that cash cushion saves the day.

The problem? Building an emergency fund can feel overwhelming — like one more thing you're failing at. Not here. In this chapter, we're building your safety net the low-stress, snack-friendly way: small steps, smart tricks, and zero guilt.

Start with $100, Not $1000 – Shrink the Mountain

When you hear "save $1000 for emergencies," it's easy to curl up in a ball and order pizza instead. So don't start there. Start with $100.

This section shows you how setting smaller goals builds momentum—and how $100 can quietly change everything.

- **Hack #316: Micro Goal Magic**

Focus on your first $100, not your first $1000. Achievable goals = faster wins.

- **Hack #317: Emergency Starter Jar**

Physically stash your first $100 in cash somewhere safe. Visual wins matter.

- **Hack #318: Celebrate the First Milestone**

Throw a tiny celebration when you hit $100. Motivation loves rewards.

- **Hack #319: Build Confidence, Not Pressure**

Every dollar saved proves you can do it. Confidence compounds.

- **Hack #320: Next Goal: $250 Party**

After $100, aim for $250. Keep the mountain broken into snack-sized pieces.

Where to Park Your Emergency Fund – Hide It (But Not Too Well)

Emergency money needs to be safe, easy to grab, but not so easy that you "accidentally" spend it on concert tickets.

This section shows you where to stash your fund so it's ready when you need it — but invisible when you don't.

- **Hack #321: Separate High-Yield Savings Account**

Keep emergency cash away from your daily banking account. Distance = discipline.

- **Hack #322: No Debit Card Linked**

Make accessing your emergency fund slightly inconvenient. Friction saves money.

- **Hack #323: Avoid Investment Risks**

Emergency funds belong somewhere boring (savings, not stocks). Stability over flash.

- **Hack #324: Nickname Your Account**

Label it something serious like "Life Happens Fund" or "Safety Net." Your brain will treat it with more respect.

- **Hack #325: Visual Dashboard Boost**

If your bank app allows it, display your emergency fund separately to see it grow every time you log in.

Automation: Your Secret Weapon – Build Without Thinking

You don't need heroic willpower to build your emergency fund—you need automation. Robots are way better savers than tired humans.

This section shows you how to automate your way to a cushy safety net without lifting a finger after setup.

- **Hack #326: Auto-Transfer on Payday**

Set a tiny auto-transfer to your emergency fund the same day you get paid. Invisible saving = winning.

- **Hack #327: Round-Up Apps for Bonus Boosts**

Apps that round up purchases and send the change to savings build extra padding without noticing.

- **Hack #328: Incremental Increase Trick**

Every three months, bump up your auto-transfer by $5–$10. It stays painless but grows fast.

- **Hack #329: Split Direct Deposits**

If possible, have part of your paycheck sent directly to savings. No middleman temptation.

- **Hack #330: Monthly Review and Tiny Tweaks**

Glance at your automation once a month. Tiny adjustments now = big impacts later.

Fun Ways to Boost Savings – Trick Your Brain into Loving It

Saving doesn't have to feel like detention. If you make it playful, you'll stick with it longer—and actually enjoy the process.

This section shows you sneaky, fun ways to grow your emergency fund without feeling like you're grounded.

- **Hack #331: Savings Bingo**

Create a bingo board with savings challenges ($10 saved, skipped takeout, sold something online). Reward yourself when you hit bingo.

- **Hack #332: Coin Jar Jackpot**

Challenge yourself to fill a coin jar. It's low effort but super satisfying.

- **Hack #333: Side Hustle Sprints**

Pick up a tiny side hustle (dog walking, selling crafts) and throw 100% of it into your fund.

- **Hack #334: No-Spend Weekend Rewards**

Every no-spend weekend earns you a $10–$20 transfer to your emergency stash.

- **Hack #335: Savings Buddy Challenges**

Find a friend. Race to see who can save $100 first. Loser buys coffee (cheaply).

What Counts as an Emergency – Defining Your "Break Glass" Moments

Not every inconvenience is a five-alarm emergency. If you don't define "emergency" clearly, it's too easy to raid your fund for concert tickets or spontaneous road trips.

This section helps you set clear, guilt-free rules for when it's okay to break into your emergency stash.

- **Hack #336: True Emergencies Only Rule**

Job loss, medical bills, car breakdowns = yes. New TV sale = absolutely not.

- **Hack #337: Create a Quick-Check List**

Write down what qualifies as an emergency for you. Reference it before touching the fund.

- **Hack #338: Sleep-On-It Rule**

If you're unsure whether something counts as an emergency, sleep on it. Urgent panic fades fast.

- **Hack #339: Separate Annoyances from Emergencies**

Flat tire = emergency. Wanting new tires because they're cooler? Not so much.

- **Hack #340: Emergency Fund Guilt-Free Use**

If it's truly an emergency, use the fund with zero guilt. That's what it's there for.

Rebuilding After Using Your Fund – Recovery Plans That Don't Suck

One of the best (and worst) moments: when you've used your emergency fund successfully... but now it's empty. Good news: rebuilding doesn't have to feel soul-crushing.

This section teaches you how to bounce back with speed and sanity.

- **Hack #341: Emergency Fund Priority Mode**

After using it, make refilling your fund your top financial goal—before vacations or new gadgets.

- **Hack #342: Micro-Rebuilds Work**

Tiny, consistent savings ($10, $20, $50 at a time) refill the fund faster than guilt and overwhelm.

- **Hack #343: Celebrate the Win First**

You *used* your emergency fund correctly! That's a financial adulting badge, not a failure.

- **Hack #344: Use Windfalls Strategically**

Tax refund, bonus, side hustle money? Funnel a slice back into rebuilding automatically.

- **Hack #345: Track Visible Progress**

Keep a simple tracker (chart, app, sticky notes) so you can actually see the fund rising again.

Emergency Fund for Freelancers and Gig Workers – Your Bigger Safety Net

If you don't have a stable paycheck, your emergency fund needs to work overtime to keep you feeling safe.

This section shows how freelancers and gig workers can build bigger, smarter cushions without living in constant terror.

- **Hack #346: Double Down Goal**

Aim for 6–9 months' worth of basic expenses instead of the usual 3–6 months.

- **Hack #347: Base Budget for Bare Bones**

Know your survival number (rent, food, insurance) so you know exactly how much you need.

- **Hack #348: Squirrel Mode in Good Seasons**

When gigs are hot, save aggressively. Winter is always coming.

- **Hack #349: Separate "Business Emergencies"**

If you're self-employed, keep a second mini-emergency fund for business-specific disasters.

- **Hack #350: Emergency Credit Buffer**

In addition to cash, keep a low-balance credit card for true business emergencies only.

Why Emergency Funds Beat Credit Cards – The Invisible Safety Superpower

Credit cards can feel like emergency plans… until you realize debt creates second emergencies. Real cash beats plastic panic every time.

This section shows why building your own fund is smarter, safer, and cheaper than relying on "just charging it."

- **Hack #351: Debt Stacks Fast**

A $500 emergency on a 20% APR card balloons to $600+ fast if you can't pay it off immediately.

- **Hack #352: Cash = Power and Peace**

Having cash ready removes panic and powerlessness from surprise crises.

- **Hack #353: No Interest Fees Stealing Your Sleep**

Every dollar in your emergency fund is a dollar you don't owe anyone later.

- **Hack #354: Avoid the Double Emergency Spiral**

One crisis is hard. A crisis plus new debt is way harder. Break the cycle.

- **Hack #355: Emergency Fund = Freedom Fund**

Cash in the bank means you have options — and options mean you're never trapped.

Tiny Everyday Habits That Feed Your Fund – Guilt-Free Growth

You don't have to "budget harder" to build your emergency fund faster. Sometimes, sneaky little habits do the work for you.

This section is packed with micro-habits that quietly fatten up your savings without feeling like punishment.

- **Hack #356: Round Up and Save Apps**

Let your bank or an app round up every purchase and sweep the change into savings.

- **Hack #357: Cash-Back Redirect Trick**

Every time you earn cashback or loyalty rewards, send them straight into your emergency fund.

- **Hack #358: Payday Skim Move**

Skim $5–$20 off every paycheck immediately, before you even start spending.

- **Hack #359: Refunds and Rebates Reboot**

Treat refunds, rebates, and surprise money like "found money" for your emergency fund.

- **Hack #360: "Would Have Spent It" Transfers**

Skipped a takeout night or returned a pair of shoes? Transfer what you *would* have spent into savings.

Mastering Everyday Money Moves

Daily habits that quietly make your wallet heavier and your stress lighter.

Big money wins are awesome — but it's the tiny, boring, daily moves that quietly stack up to change your whole financial life. Smart habits aren't about grand gestures. They're about subtle tweaks that work in the background, while you keep living your regular, awesome life.

This chapter is all about those sneaky, everyday shortcuts that don't require a new personality, a 6-figure income, or a color-coded spreadsheet. Just a few tweaks to your normal routines — and suddenly, your wallet is a little fatter, your stress is a little lighter, and Future You is doing a happy dance.

Meal Planning for Savings – Food Without the Budget Hangover

Food is one of the fastest ways money disappears — but also one of the fastest ways you can take control again. Meal planning doesn't mean eating sad salads for eternity. It means making tiny, strategic choices that leave your wallet (and your belly) way happier.

This section shows how a few easy tweaks can slash grocery costs, kill food waste, and still keep dinner feeling exciting, not depressing.

- Hack #361: Plan Before You Shop

A quick 10-minute plan before hitting the store saves you serious cash — and snack-driven regret.

- **Hack #362: Master the Leftovers Remix**

Plan meals that turn into other meals (think roast chicken into tacos). Less waste, more deliciousness.

- **Hack #363: Theme Nights Save Sanity**

Taco Tuesday, Pasta Thursday — repeating themes cuts decision fatigue and random overspending.

- **Hack #364: The Half-List Trick**

Make your grocery list — then cut it in half. You usually don't need as much as you think.

- **Hack #365: First In, First Out**

Use up the oldest stuff in your fridge first. It's like playing a weird survival game, but for your budget.

Saving on Utilities Without Freezing – Comfort and Cash Wins

Saving on utilities doesn't mean living in a parka indoors. It means being just a little smarter about energy use without sacrificing your Netflix marathons or hot showers.

This section helps you trim down those power, water, and heating bills — and still feel fully alive and cozy.

- **Hack #366: Thermostat Ninja Moves**

Adjusting your thermostat by just 1–2 degrees saves a surprising amount over a year.

- **Hack #367: Layer Up Before Cranking Heat**

Throw on a hoodie before you touch the thermostat. Instant warmth, zero dollars.

- **Hack #368: Water Heater Check**

Lower your water heater to 120°F (about 49°C) — safer, cheaper, and you'll never notice.

- **Hack #369: Unplug Energy Vampires**

Chargers, TVs, and random devices suck power even when "off." Unplug or use power strips.

- **Hack #370: Laundry Efficiency Wins**

Wash clothes in cold water and air-dry when possible. Clothes last longer, bills shrink.

DIY Repairs That Actually Work – Fix It, Don't Fling It

You don't need to be Bob the Builder to pull off small repairs that save you hundreds. Thanks to YouTube and common sense, basic DIY can be a total financial superpower.

This section shows how small fixes add up — and why fearlessly grabbing a wrench now and then is pure wallet magic.

- **Hack #371: YouTube Before You Yelp**

Before calling a pro, search YouTube for DIY fixes. Sometimes a $5 part beats a $200 service call.

- **Hack #372: Toolbox Starter Pack**

A hammer, screwdriver set, duct tape, and a plunger solve 80% of beginner emergencies.

- **Hack #373: Patch, Don't Pitch**

Ripped clothes, scratched furniture, broken jewelry — tons of stuff is easily repairable if you try.

- **Hack #374: Learn One Skill a Month**

Focus on mastering one basic fix each month — changing a tire, fixing a leaky tap, sewing a button.

- **Hack #375: Celebrate the Wins**

Even a basic fix deserves a mini celebration. DIY confidence compounds fast.

Free Entertainment That Feels Luxe – Fun Without the Swipe

Entertainment doesn't have to mean expensive concerts, overpriced restaurants, or $20 cocktails. Fun can be free — or close to it — without feeling like you're settling for boredom.

This section shows you how to load up your social calendar without draining your bank account.

- **Hack #376: Local Free Events Scan**

Every city has free festivals, outdoor movies, museum days, or markets. Check community boards weekly.

- **Hack #377: Potluck Party Magic**

Host friends for potlucks or board game nights. Everyone brings something, no one breaks the bank.

- **Hack #378: Library Goldmine**

Libraries aren't just books anymore — think free movies, workshops, speakers, even tool rentals.

- **Hack #379: Nature Adventures**

Parks, hikes, beaches, public gardens — built-in entertainment, zero admission fees.

- **Hack #380: Master the Free Trial Circuit**

Test out new classes, apps, and memberships with free trials — just set calendar reminders to cancel!

Financial Hygiene Habits to Lock In – Maintenance Mode Wins

Building wealth isn't just about big moves. It's about keeping your financial health tidy with tiny, boring, invisible wins stacked up daily.

This section teaches you easy financial hygiene habits that keep everything flowing smoothly — no panic attacks required.

- **Hack #381: Weekly Money Glances**

Spend 5–10 minutes once a week peeking at your balances and upcoming bills. Awareness = control.

- **Hack #382: Track One Tiny Metric**

Pick one thing to watch: savings rate, debt payoff, spending on groceries. Focus beats overwhelm.

- **Hack #383: Auto-Pay the Essentials**

Put bills on auto-pay to avoid late fees — and free up brain space for better stuff.

- **Hack #384: Delete Temptation Emails**

Unsubscribe from shopping newsletters. No ad = no impulsive buys.

- **Hack #385: Monthly Mini-Audits**

Once a month, glance through your spending. One quick sweep catches leaks before they become floods.

Grocery Hacks That Stretch Your Dollars – Smart Cart Wins

Groceries eat a huge part of your budget — but with a few tricks, you can feed yourself better for way less.

This section teaches you stealth moves to crush your grocery bill without turning into a coupon extremist.

- **Hack #386: Shop the Edges**

The outer aisles (produce, dairy, meat) are cheaper and healthier than the center snack vortex.

- **Hack #387: Generic Brands FTW**

Most store brands come from the same factories as name brands. Try swapping and bank the savings.

- **Hack #388: Cash Envelope Trick**

Take cash only to the store. When the money's gone, the shopping stops.

- **Hack #389: Buy In-Season or Frozen**

In-season produce is way cheaper and tastier. Off-season? Go frozen instead of overpriced imports.

- **Hack #390: Leftover Day = Money Day**

Dedicate one dinner a week to eating random leftovers. It's like Iron Chef, but cheaper.

Transportation Savings Without Sacrificing Freedom – Wheels on a Budget

Getting around doesn't have to cost you half your paycheck. A few clever transportation tricks can save you serious cash while keeping your freedom intact.

This section gives you simple ways to cut travel costs without feeling trapped at home.

- **Hack #391: Carpool Opportunist**

Even one shared ride a week cuts fuel and wear-and-tear costs down noticeably.

- **Hack #392: Walk/Bike the Short Trips**

Short drives = huge gas waste. Walk or bike errands under 2km (or a mile) when possible.

- **Hack #393: Public Transport Test Runs**

Even switching one commute a week to bus/train saves gas and parking costs.

- **Hack #394: Bundle Errands Together**

One big outing for groceries, post office, gym = one fuel-efficient day instead of three.

- **Hack #395: Telecommute Days**

Negotiate even one work-from-home day if possible. Savings on gas + time = double win.

Money Mindfulness Without the Woo-Woo – Conscious Spending Wins

You don't need to meditate on a mountaintop to be mindful about your money. Mindfulness here just means paying attention — and spending with intention.

This section shows how tiny awareness tweaks massively improve your money habits without requiring a total lifestyle overhaul.

- **Hack #396: Pause Before You Purchase**

Before you buy, pause 10 seconds and ask, "Do I actually want this, or am I bored/hungry/stressed?"

- **Hack #397: One-Click Barriers**

Disable one-click shopping on apps. Tiny extra steps create smart hesitation.

- **Hack #398: Wishlist It First**

Add non-urgent wants to a 30-day wishlist. If you still want it after 30 days, buy it guilt-free.

- **Hack #399: Focus on Value, Not Price**

Ask, "Is this worth it?" instead of just "Is this cheap?" Quality > endless replacement cycles.

- **Hack #400: Daily Money Gratitude**

Once a day, notice one thing your money made possible (a meal, a bill paid, a cozy bed). Appreciation strengthens discipline.

Lifestyle Upgrades That Don't Break the Bank

How to feel richer without actually spending richer.

You don't need to win the lottery or marry a billionaire to live a little fancier. Feeling richer is way more about *how* you spend your money than *how much* you have. It's about sneaky little upgrades that make your daily life feel smoother, comfier, and more fun — without wrecking your bank account.

This chapter is packed with easy lifestyle boosts you can make today. No luxury yachts required. Just smart, low-cost switches that make every day feel a little more "I'm thriving" and a lot less "I'm barely surviving."

Small Home Upgrades – Cozy, Classy, and Cheap

You don't need a total home renovation to upgrade your space. Tiny, strategic tweaks can make your home feel like a boutique hotel without the boutique bill.

This section shows you how to get major vibe upgrades with minor cash outlays.

- **Hack #401: Lighting Mood Boost**

Swap harsh bulbs for soft white or warm LED lighting. Instantly cozy, instantly better.

- **Hack #402: Throw Blanket Trick**

One cozy throw blanket = immediate "fancy living room" effect. Bonus if it's textured.

- **Hack #403: Scent Upgrade**

Candles, diffusers, or even simmering cinnamon on the stove make your home feel expensive for cheap.

- **Hack #404: Declutter Like You Mean It**

Nothing feels richer than clean surfaces. Free, fast, and powerful.

- **Hack #405: Fresh Towels and Bedding**

A new towel or set of sheets = instant daily luxury for under $50.

Fun "Budget-Friendly Bougie" Habits – Feel Fancy Without Feeling Broke

Sometimes it's not what you buy — it's how you treat yourself. "Budget bougie" means adding small moments of luxury without spending like royalty.

This section shows how to sprinkle a little "treat yourself" into everyday life.

- **Hack #406: Fancy Glassware Rule**

Drink water or juice out of your best wine glass. It's ridiculous. It's amazing.

- **Hack #407: At-Home Spa Days**

Face masks, DIY pedicures, bubble baths — luxury is a vibe, not a price tag.

- **Hack #408: Coffee Shop Rituals at Home**

Make your coffee a whole experience with frothy milk, cinnamon, and a real mug.

- **Hack #409: Plate It Pretty**

Even leftovers look like gourmet meals if you plate them nicely.

- **Hack #410: Fancy Pajama Policy**

Upgrade your pajamas. Feeling good at home is pure luxury.

Affordable Self-Care – Real Recharge Without the Price Tag

Self-care doesn't have to mean $300 spa days or $50 yoga mats. True self-care is about feeling restored, not just posting about it.

This section teaches you how to build real self-care habits that don't nuke your wallet.

- **Hack #411: Nature Therapy**

A walk in the park or a hike costs nothing — and resets your brain better than a day at a resort.

- **Hack #412: DIY Face Masks and Scrubs**

Honey, oatmeal, sugar scrubs — homemade spa magic for pennies.

- **Hack #413: Free Yoga and Meditation Apps**

YouTube is packed with free workouts, meditation guides, and breathwork sessions.

- **Hack #414: Library = Wellness Center**

Libraries have free workshops, calming spaces, and even art supplies sometimes.

- **Hack #415: Phone-Free Hours**

The richest feeling ever: time away from screens. Costs $0, saves sanity.

Smart Splurges That Stretch Happiness – Big Joys, Tiny Prices

Some splurges are actually smart investments in your daily happiness — when you pick the right ones.

This section shows how to splurge wisely and make the happiness last way longer.

- **Hack #416: Upgrade One Daily Essential**

A better pillow, headphones, or water bottle you use every day = best ROI on comfort.

- **Hack #417: Buy Experiences, Not Stuff**

Concert tickets, a weekend road trip, or a cooking class = memories > material junk.

- **Hack #418: Subscription Swaps**

Swap out subscriptions you never use for ones that bring real joy — music, books, learning.

- **Hack #419: Invest in Hobby Tools**

Buy the better paintbrush, running shoes, or guitar strings. Hobbies are happiness multipliers.

- **Hack #420: Tiny Indulgences**

Small luxuries like premium tea, a fancy soap, or a nice pen elevate your daily grind.

High-Impact, Low-Cost Changes – Tiny Tweaks, Big Feel-Good

Some upgrades don't cost much at all — but they seriously change how you experience your life, your space, and even your mindset.

This section gives you high-impact moves that are cheap (or free) but make you feel like you just leveled up.

- **Hack #421: Rearrange Your Furniture**

A room shuffle feels like a makeover — for $0.

- **Hack #422: Create a "Happy Corner"**

Designate a cozy nook with books, lights, or plants. Instant sanctuary.

- **Hack #423: Daily Music Upgrade**

Blast a good playlist while you cook, clean, or work. Good soundtracks = good vibes.

- **Hack #424: Start a Tiny Garden**

Even a few herbs on a windowsill make life feel more abundant.

- **Hack #425: Fresh Flowers Rule**

Buy yourself a $5 bunch of flowers at the grocery store. Weekly. Non-negotiable.

Wardrobe Tweaks That Feel Rich – Dress Like You Mean It

Looking good doesn't require designer labels. Smart wardrobe tweaks can make you feel sharper, more confident — and richer — without maxing out your card.

This section shows you how to upgrade your style game the smart, sneaky way.

- **Hack #426: Fit Beats Price**

Well-fitted clothes look 10x more expensive than ill-fitting expensive ones.

- **Hack #427: Signature Look Shortcut**

Find one "you" outfit formula and lean into it. Consistency = effortless cool.

- **Hack #428: Accessory Magic**

A sharp belt, bold earrings, or a classic watch upgrades even basic outfits.

- **Hack #429: Shoe Shine Rule**

Polish your shoes. Worn-down, dirty shoes kill a good outfit instantly.

- **Hack #430: Secondhand Treasure Hunts**

Thrift stores and online resale shops = designer vibes for budget prices.

Mini Travel Upgrades Without the Huge Costs – Explore Smarter

Traveling feels luxurious — but you don't need five-star resorts to feel like you're living the dream.

This section shows how to upgrade your travel experiences while keeping your wallet happily intact.

- **Hack #431: Midweek Getaways**

Hotels and flights are cheaper midweek. Plus, fewer crowds = fancier vibes.

- **Hack #432: Local Adventures First**

Explore nearby towns, nature parks, or museums. You don't have to go far to feel like you're traveling.

- **Hack #433: Loyalty Points Play**

Sign up for free hotel and airline loyalty programs to rack up freebies and upgrades faster.

- **Hack #434: Picnic Over Restaurant**

Picnic with local goodies = gourmet meal for cheap — and often with a better view.

- **Hack #435: Pack Like a Pro**

A well-packed bag (snacks, entertainment, chargers) saves you from expensive impulse buys on the road.

Upgraded Foodie Life Without the High Bill – Gourmet on a Budget

Eating well feels fancy — but you can enjoy chef-level meals without blowing your budget on takeout.

This section shows you how to make your foodie dreams happen affordably.

- **Hack #436: Farmer's Market Power**

Shop at local farmer's markets close to closing time for discounts on fresh goodies.

- **Hack #437: DIY "Fancy" Meals**

Master a few impressive-looking recipes (hello, homemade pizza!) that are way cheaper than restaurant versions.

- **Hack #438: Cooking Challenges**

Challenge yourself to create a "restaurant dish" using only pantry basics. Winner gets bragging rights.

- **Hack #439: Brunch at Home**

Make a lavish weekend brunch at home instead of dropping $50 at a café.

- **Hack #440: Food Swap Parties**

Host potluck food swaps with friends. Everyone brings something — and you feast for cheap.

Little Luxuries You Should Say Yes To – Permission to Enjoy

Money isn't just for surviving — it's for living. Some "unnecessary" purchases are actually ridiculously necessary for your soul.

This section gives you permission to say yes to small splurges that bring disproportionate joy.

- **Hack #441: Favorite Candle Splurge**

A great-smelling candle turns even a Tuesday night into a cozy celebration.

- **Hack #442: Art and Beauty at Home**

A $10 poster, a framed photo, or a piece of DIY art = endless smiles per dollar.

- **Hack #443: Super Comfy Socks**

Life's too short for scratchy, sad socks. Upgrade. Trust me.

- **Hack #444: Fresh Journal or Notebook**

New pages = new ideas. Totally justifiable.

- **Hack #445: Tiny Celebrations**

Say yes to cupcakes, confetti, and random toast-worthy wins. You're allowed.

Resetting After a Money Mistake

How to bounce back fast when you mess up (because you will, and it's fine).

Here's the thing: you're going to mess up with money sometimes. Everyone does — even the people who look like they have it all together on Instagram. The difference isn't whether you screw up. It's how you recover.

This chapter is your toolkit for bouncing back fast, without guilt, shame, or giving up. Mistakes aren't proof you're bad with money — they're proof you're in the game. Let's learn how to shake it off, reset like a pro, and keep moving forward.

First Response to a Financial Screw-Up – The No-Panic Playbook

The moment you realize you made a money mistake, it's easy to spiral into guilt or freeze up. Neither helps. Your first response matters more than the mistake itself.

This section shows you how to respond smartly instead of emotionally — and start repairing right away.

- **Hack #446: Pause, Don't Panic**

Take a deep breath. Money mistakes feel bigger in the moment than they actually are.

- **Hack #447: Name the Mistake**

Get clear: overspent? Missed a bill? Investment regret? Label it — clarity is calming.

- **Hack #448: Separate Feelings from Facts**

Feeling bad isn't the same as being bad. Focus on what actually happened, not what your brain is yelling.

- **Hack #449: Assess the Real Damage**

Write down exactly how much you lost, overspent, or need to fix. Numbers feel less scary than vague panic.

- **Hack #450: Plan Before Punishing**

You don't need to punish yourself. You need a next step. Focus forward.

Quick Recovery Checklist – Your Fast-Action Reset

Once you spot a mistake, the faster you act, the less damage it causes. This is your emergency checklist for bouncing back before things snowball.

This section gives you a no-drama, no-shame action plan.

- **Hack #451: Plug the Leak**

Stop the mistake from continuing (cancel the subscription, return the impulse buy, freeze the credit card).

- **Hack #452: Cover the Immediate Hole**

If you overspent rent money, shuffle savings or side cash fast. Prioritize essentials.

- **Hack #453: Contact Companies Early**

Late on a payment? Call them. Early honesty usually leads to waived fees or better plans.

- **Hack #454: Set a 7-Day Correction Goal**

Give yourself one week to patch the mistake. Speed > perfection.

- **Hack #455: Forgive + Adjust**

Mistakes don't need marathons of guilt. Correct course and keep moving.

Rebuilding Momentum After Setbacks – Keep the Engine Running

The real danger after a mistake isn't the money — it's losing momentum. Quitting because of one screw-up is like slashing three tires because you got one flat.

This section shows you how to rebuild momentum fast and stay in the game.

- **Hack #456: Micro-Wins Mindset**

Stack tiny victories (paid one bill? skipped one coffee?) to rebuild confidence fast.

- **Hack #457: Daily Reset Ritual**

Each morning, mentally reset: "Today, I make one smart money move." One at a time.

- **Hack #458: Streak Saver Moves**

Track streaks — days paying attention to money, days saving a little. Streaks rebuild power.

- **Hack #459: Focus on the Next Step Only**

Ignore the giant mountain ahead. What's the next single smart move? Do that.

- **Hack #460: Celebrate Progress Loudly**

Every small fix is a win. Loudly. Brag to Future You

Forgiveness > Guilt – Why Shame Doesn't Pay Your Bills

Feeling guilty about a money mistake might feel like the responsible thing to do — but guilt doesn't fix your budget. Forgiveness clears the road so you can actually drive forward.

This section helps you swap guilt for grace and speed up your financial healing.

- **Hack #461: Guilt is a Financial Sinkhole**

The more time you spend feeling guilty, the less energy you have to fix and grow.

- **Hack #462: Talk to Yourself Like a Friend**

If your best friend made this mistake, you wouldn't scream at them. Talk to yourself the same way.

- **Hack #463: Mistakes Don't Define You**

Your worst financial day isn't your whole story. It's one weird chapter. Keep writing.

- **Hack #464: Visualize the Bounce-Back**

Picture yourself six months from now: steady, stronger, moving on. Make that vision louder than your guilt.

- **Hack #465: Build a Mistake Manual**

Write down what you learned from each mistake. Turning it into a manual = turning pain into power.

Mistakes as Part of the Long Game – Play to Win, Not to Be Perfect

Real financial success isn't about never messing up. It's about building resilience and momentum even when you do.

This section reframes mistakes as necessary, normal steps on the road to winning long-term.

- **Hack #466: Normalize the Misstep**

Every financially successful person has messed up — overspent, made bad investments, impulse-splurged.

- **Hack #467: Fail Faster, Recover Faster**

Mess up, fix it, learn. Repeat. The faster you cycle, the stronger you get.

- **Hack #468: Zoom Out Timeline Trick**

In 5 years, will you even remember this mistake? Probably not. Keep perspective.

- **Hack #469: Mistakes = Data**

Every mistake gives you new info about your triggers, habits, and blind spots.

- **Hack #470: You're Still in the Game**

As long as you're still making moves, you're still winning. Game on.

Building a Mistake Buffer – Prepare for Next Time (Because I t'll Happen)

Future mistakes are inevitable — so why not build cushions now to soften the fall?

This section shows how to pre-build mistake buffers so future you has less stress and faster recoveries.

- **Hack #471: Micro Emergency Fund**

Have a mini fund (even $100) for "Oops, I messed up" moments. It's emotional insurance.

- **Hack #472: Backup Plan Playbook**

Create mini scripts: If X happens (overspend, late bill), I do Y (call company, use fund, reset budget).

- **Hack #473: Slow Money Moves Rule**

Wait 24 hours before major purchases. Slowing down = fewer impulsive regrets.

- **Hack #474: Auto-Save Tiny Wins**

Auto-saving small amounts regularly cushions future mistakes effortlessly.

- **Hack #475: Permission to Course-Correct**

Write yourself a literal note: "I'm allowed to fix mistakes without quitting."

Identifying Your Money Triggers – Spot the Pattern, Break the Cycle

Most money mistakes aren't random. They usually follow patterns — stress spending, FOMO, boredom buying. If you spot your triggers, you can dodge way more mistakes before they happen.

This section shows how to recognize your financial kryptonite and build smarter defenses.

- **Hack #476: Mood Check Before You Swipe**

Before a big purchase, check your emotional state. Hungry, angry, lonely, tired = danger zones.

- **Hack #477: Spending Log Reality Check**

Keep a tiny spending log for a week. Patterns will pop fast.

- **Hack #478: Trigger Tracker Notes**

After a money mistake, jot down what you were feeling, doing, and thinking. Instant pattern spotting.

- **Hack #479: Replace, Don't Just Resist**

Swap your go-to bad habit (online shopping) with a good one (walk, journal, playlist).

- **Hack #480: Pre-Build Alternatives**

Make a list of "instead" activities for your top money triggers. (Instead of shopping: call a friend, hit a free museum.)

When to Get Help – Smart Moves, Not Weakness

Sometimes bouncing back after a mistake means calling in reinforcements — a financial coach, a therapist, or just an honest friend.

This section teaches you when (and how) to ask for help without feeling embarrassed.

- **Hack #481: Normalize the Help Call**

Financial pros exist because everyone needs help sometimes. It's a smart move, not a failure.

- **Hack #482: Accountability Buddy Power**

Team up with a friend to check in weekly. No judgment, just support and progress.

- **Hack #483: Free Financial Counseling**

Nonprofits often offer free or low-cost financial advice. It's not just for "big messes."

- **Hack #484: Therapy Isn't Just for Trauma**

If money stress triggers bigger emotional spirals, talking to a therapist can reset everything.

- **Hack #485: Early Help > Emergency Help**

Ask for help early. It's way easier to tweak a small problem than rescue a total crash.

Mistake-Proofing Your Future Moves – Gentle Armor

You can't avoid all mistakes forever — but you can armor up in ways that make future errors smaller, cheaper, and less stressful.

This section gives you a mini toolbelt for future-proofing your financial life.

- **Hack #486: Budget Breathing Room**

Build wiggle room into your budget. Every dollar of flex space reduces future panic.

- **Hack #487: Mistake Savings Line Item**

Budget a tiny "oops" line every month — $10–$50 — for unplanned facepalms.

- **Hack #488: Snooze Buttons for Spending**

Set alerts for bill due dates, subscription renewals, and auto-drafts. Sleep on decisions before spending.

- **Hack #489: Guilt-Free Reset Days**

Schedule a monthly "reset day" where you audit your money, fix leaks, and clean up without judgment.

- **Hack #490: Mistake Story Retell Rule**

When you talk about your mistake, tell it like a success story: "I caught it early, I fixed it, and I'm smarter now."

Saving for Fun: Goals That Make You Smile

Why saving for joy is just as important as saving for emergencies.

Saving money isn't just about building financial armor for disasters. It's also about building a life that makes you *want* to get out of bed every morning. Emergency funds are essential — but so are dream funds, splurge stashes, and celebration accounts. Money isn't just for safety. It's for living.

This chapter is about saving on purpose — for the stuff that lights you up. Whether it's trips, hobbies, surprise parties, or just making regular Tuesdays feel a little extra special, saving for joy isn't irresponsible. It's smart. Let's design a money plan that feeds your soul as much as it feeds your bank account.

Dream Funds – Building Your Big Beautiful Someday

You don't have to wait for "someday" to start moving toward your dream life. Dream funds are how you get there — one tiny deposit at a time.

This section shows you how to create targeted savings for the adventures, experiences, and life upgrades you actually want.

- **Hack #491: Name It to Claim It**

Label your dream fund something exciting: "Paris Adventure" or "Home Studio" instead of just "Savings."

- **Hack #492: Dream Board Deposits**

Every time you add money to your dream fund, add a new picture or note to your vision board.

- **Hack #493: Progress Thermometer Magic**

Track your dream fund with a fun visual you can color in. Watching it grow builds momentum.

- **Hack #494: Micro-Dream Goals**

Break big dreams into tiny milestones. Celebrate every $100 closer.

- **Hack #495: Weekly Dream Money Habit**

Deposit a small amount every week — even $5 — toward your dream. It keeps the dream alive and moving.

Celebration Funds – Save for Joy, Not Just Survival

Everyday life is full of tiny victories worth celebrating — and having a stash ready makes it easier to party guilt-free.

This section helps you set up a dedicated Celebration Fund so you can toast your wins without torching your budget.

- **Hack #496: Milestone Party Planning**

Set small savings goals tied to milestones: new job, finishing a project, paying off a card.

- **Hack #497: Celebration Wishlist**

Create a list of fun, affordable ways to celebrate — fancy dinners, staycations, spa days at home.

- **Hack #498: Micro-Rewards Matter**

Save for tiny celebrations like surviving a tough week, finishing a book, or just showing up.

- **Hack #499: Guilt-Free Party Budget**

Plan the celebration fund ahead so you can splurge joyfully, not stressfully.

- **Hack #500: Friend Fund Challenge**

Get friends involved — everyone saves $10 a month toward a group celebration fund.

Vacation Savings Hacks – Travel Smarter, Smile Bigger

Vacations aren't irresponsible splurges — they're memory-makers. But they're way more fun when you're not paying them off months later.

This section shows you how to build a vacation savings plan that leaves you relaxed before, during, and after the trip.

- **Hack #501: Destination Jar**

Have a physical or digital jar labeled with your dream destination. Seeing it keeps you motivated.

- **Hack #502: Automatic Vacation Drafts**

Set an auto-transfer into a "Travel Fund" every paycheck — even if it's tiny.

- **Hack #503: Off-Season Wins**

Plan trips during off-peak times. It slashes costs and often makes experiences way better.

- **Hack #504: Reward Yourself with Points**

Use credit card points, loyalty programs, and travel hacks to boost your budget without boosting your spend.

- **Hack #505: Airbnb and Cheap Flight Alerts**

Follow sites that send you deals. A little planning saves you hundreds.

Guilt-Free Splurge Savings – Permission to Play

Splurging doesn't have to mean sabotaging your future. With a splurge fund, you can say "yes" without the creeping guilt monster.

This section helps you build a happy little splurge account you can use with full permission — and zero stress.

- **Hack #506: Splurge Savings Rule**

Put 5–10% of every paycheck into your splurge fund automatically.

- **Hack #507: Impulse Control Button**

If you want something big, sleep on it — then check your splurge fund. If you've got it, guilt-free go time.

- **Hack #508: Big Buy Wishlist**

Keep a running list of dream buys. Prioritize and save accordingly.

- **Hack #509: Fun-First Fridays**

Every payday Friday, toss a few bucks into your splurge fund before paying anything else.

- **Hack #510: Micro-Upgrade Moments**

Use splurge funds for tiny upgrades: premium coffee, better sheets, nicer headphones.

Designing a Life You're Excited About – Big Picture Money Moves

Saving isn't just about not drowning — it's about designing a life that actually *excites* you to live it. Your money should build the version of your life that makes you happiest, not just the safest.

This section helps you think bigger about saving for the life you actually want — not the one you feel stuck with.

- **Hack #511: The "Perfect Day" Exercise**

Write out your perfect regular day. Then start saving for the pieces you don't have yet.

- **Hack #512: Save for Freedom, Not Just Stuff**

Savings can buy days off, slow mornings, side businesses — not just more junk.

- **Hack #513: Future Life Funding Account**

Set up a savings account specifically for future dreams: career change, moving cities, taking a gap year.

- **Hack #514: Memory Over Materials Rule**

When choosing between saving for an object or an experience, lean experience. Memories appreciate in value.

- **Hack #515: Joy-Based Budgeting**

Assign savings goals to things that genuinely spark joy — not what looks good on Instagram.

Mini-Dream Funds for Small Joys – Everyday Magic

Not every dream has to be a world tour. Sometimes it's a weekend getaway, a new guitar, or a surprise day off — mini-dreams matter too.

This section shows you how saving for small joys keeps motivation high and life way more fun.

- **Hack #516: Micro-Dream Wishlist**

Make a list of $50–$500 dreams. Cheaper, faster wins build momentum.

- **Hack #517: Small-Goal Celebration Rule**

Celebrate every mini-dream you hit — it reinforces your ability to win.

- **Hack #518: "Under $100" Challenges**

Challenge yourself to create a dream experience for under $100 — and save toward it.

- **Hack #519: Stack the Small Wins**

Hitting three mini-dreams boosts your happiness more than one giant one sometimes.

- **Hack #520: Quarterly Dream Funds**

Every three months, pick a new mini-dream and build a tiny fund toward it.

Secret Savings Stashes – Build Fun Into the Budget

Having hidden pockets of money for fun can make the tightest budgets feel way more expansive and exciting.

This section shows you how to sneak secret fun money into your savings plan without sabotaging essentials.

- **Hack #521: Cash Envelope Surprise**

Tuck $5–$20 into a random envelope each week. Open them for a guilt-free treat later.

- **Hack #522: Hidden App Accounts**

Use apps that create hidden savings by rounding up or micro-saving without you noticing.

- **Hack #523: Surprise Me Jar**

Throw random leftover cash into a "Surprise Me" jar — then do something random and fun with it.

- **Hack #524: Side Hustle Fun Funds**

If you pick up a micro-gig (like surveys or small tasks), toss that money into a pure fun fund.

- **Hack #525: Birthday Money Boost**

Every year, save part of any birthday or holiday cash for something ridiculous and joyful.

Emotional Safety Nets – Saving for the Heart, Not Just the Wallet

Money isn't just protection against bills — it can also be protection for your emotional life. Saving for emotional safety nets (breakups, bad days, reinvention periods) is wildly powerful.

This section teaches you how to emotionally bulletproof yourself with money.

- **Hack #526: Bad Day Escape Fund**

Save for spontaneous nights out, spa days, or trips when life punches you.

- **Hack #527: Restart Fund**

Build a small fund dedicated to "starting over" if you ever need it — new city, new job, fresh chapter.

- **Hack #528: Comfort Purchases Permission**

Saving for comfort items — a cozy hoodie, a nostalgic book — gives you healthy outlets.

- **Hack #529: Bridge Funds for Life Gaps**

Save so you can take time off during mental health dips, career pivots, or unexpected losses.

- **Hack #530: Therapy or Coaching Buffers**

Save for mental health boosts, coaching sessions, or classes that rebuild your spirit when needed.

Turning Wins Into Habits – Keep the Joy Growing

Saving for fun isn't a one-time stunt — it's a lifestyle. When you embed joy-based saving into your normal routine, you build a life that keeps getting better.

This section shows you how to make saving for happiness part of your default mode.

- **Hack #531: Auto-Save Joy Fund**

Set it and forget it — automatic transfers into your fun accounts every payday.

- **Hack #532: Quarterly Joy Reviews**

Every three months, check in: What's bringing you joy? What dreams are next?

- **Hack #533: Celebrate Saving, Not Just Spending**

Throw mini parties when you hit savings goals — not just when you buy something.

- **Hack #534: Level Up Your Dreams**

As you hit goals, dream bigger. Your next dream is always waiting.

- **Hack #535: Stay Playful About It**

Saving for fun should always feel exciting, not stressful. If it's boring, you're doing it wrong.

Financial Self-Care: Money Moves for Your Mental Health

Because managing money *is* managing mental health.

Money stress doesn't just live in your wallet — it campfires right into your brain. Bills you can't pay, debts piling up, unexpected emergencies — they don't just hurt your finances. They quietly erode your energy, your sleep, and your ability to dream bigger.

This chapter isn't about making you feel guilty for worrying. It's about building tiny, realistic money habits that actually *lower* your stress and *boost* your calm. Managing your money well isn't about being rich — it's about protecting your peace. Let's put your mental health first without needing to meditate on a mountaintop or win the lottery.

Building a Financial Calm Routine – Your Money Peace Ritual

You brush your teeth daily to prevent chaos in your mouth. You can build simple money habits to prevent chaos in your mind, too.

This section shows you how a small, steady "money calm" routine keeps anxiety low and confidence high — without adding a ton of new homework to your life.

- **Hack #536: Weekly 5-Minute Money Peek**

Every Sunday, just glance at your bank balance. No judgment, no spreadsheets. Awareness is calming.

- **Hack #537: Safe Place for Bills**

Pick one spot (drawer, folder, app) where all your bills live. No more panicked hunting under couch cushions.

- **Hack #538: Money Wins Journal**

Once a week, jot down one money win. Even "I packed lunch once" counts.

- **Hack #539: Predictable Paydays Habit**

Always know when and where your next paycheck is coming. Predictability soothes nerves.

- **Hack #540: Quiet Payday Ritual**

Celebrate each payday by moving a tiny piece to savings before doing anything else. Calm   Confidence.

Money Anxiety Coping Tricks – Soothing the Spiral

Financial anxiety is real. It's not about being bad at money — it's about how your brain reacts to uncertainty. Good news: you can calm it down without needing to fix everything overnight.

This section gives you quick, friendly tools to catch and cool the anxiety spiral before it drags you under.

- **Hack #541: Name the Fear Out Loud**

Say it: "I'm scared I won't have enough for rent." Naming it makes it smaller.

- **Hack #542: Emergency Budget Sketch**

Create a bare-bones survival budget. Knowing your absolute minimums gives you power.

- **Hack #543: Debt Spiral Interrupts**

Instead of obsessing over your total debt, zoom in on the next $100 goal. Tiny bites kill the monster.

- **Hack #544: Gratitude Gaps**

Write down three things money *is* doing for you right now (housing, food, freedom). Reminds you you're not losing.

- **Hack #545: Financial Power Poses**

Yes, really. Strike a superhero pose for 60 seconds before checking accounts. It rewires your brain for calm.

Self-Care Spending That's Smart, Not Sabotaging – Healing, Not Hurting

Self-care sometimes gets twisted into "spend $400 on a spa day to fix your soul." Real self-care spending should heal you, not sabotage your progress.

This section teaches you how to spend on yourself wisely — and feel genuinely better afterward.

- **Hack #546: Self-Care Budget Line**

Build $10–$50 a month into your budget for real self-care: books, therapy, hobbies, mini-getaways.

- **Hack #547: Define Your Real Self-Care**

What actually recharges you? (Hint: It's not always what Instagram says.)

- **Hack #548: Planned vs. Panic Purchases**

Plan self-care treats ahead of time — not during meltdowns when spending can spiral.

- **Hack #549: Experience Over Stuff**

Experiences (massages, nature days, workshops) refill your soul longer than random stuff.

- **Hack #550: Guilt-Free Self-Care Spending**

Spending on true self-care isn't "bad" — it's emotional maintenance. Honor it.

Gentle Financial Resets – Bounce Back Without the Shame Spiral

You don't have to wait for a New Year, a new month, or some mythical perfect Monday to reset your money. Gentle, immediate resets are how you keep going without quitting.

This section gives you simple, forgiving ways to reboot your finances anytime — without shame.

- **Hack #551: The "Today Reset" Rule**

Bad money day? Cool. Reset today. No waiting, no guilt.

- **Hack #552: One Tiny Win First**

When you reset, start with one micro-win: transfer $5, check one account, cancel one charge.

- **Hack #553: Forgiveness First, Fixing Second**

Forgive the mistake *before* you try to fix it. Emotionally reset first, practically reset second.

- **Hack #554: Celebrate the Reset**

Choosing to reset is a win. Celebrate it like you just won a prize.

- **Hack #555: Resets Are Muscle Memory**

The more often you reset, the easier and faster it gets. Resilience > perfection.

Redefining "Success" with Money – Your Version, Not Theirs

Success doesn't have to mean six-figure salaries, luxury cars, or impressing strangers online. Financial self-care means building a money life that *feels good to you* — not what looks flashy to other people.

This section shows you how to define success on your own terms, so you can stop chasing someone else's dream.

- **Hack #556: Personal Joy > Public Applause**

If it doesn't make you genuinely happier, it's not your goal — even if it's "normal."

- **Hack #557: Small Successes Stack**

Paying off one small debt? Success. Packing lunch three days in a row? Success.

- **Hack #558: Comparison Detox Days**

Take regular breaks from social media money comparison traps. Your journey is yours.

- **Hack #559: Create a Personal Rich List**

Write your own "rich life" list — what truly feels abundant to *you*, not influencers.

- **Hack #560: Normalize Weird Goals**

It's okay if your dream is an herb garden and a three-day workweek instead of a yacht.

Money Boundaries = Mental Health Boundaries – Say No to Stay Sane

Protecting your money sometimes means protecting your mental health too — especially when people, companies, or temptations try to crash your plans.

This section shows how to set money boundaries firmly (and kindly) without feeling like a villain.

- **Hack #561: Budget = Boundaries on Purpose**

Your budget isn't punishment. It's a boundary you set to protect your dreams.

- **Hack #562: Pre-Script Your "No"**

Have go-to phrases ready: "That's not in my budget right now" or "I'm focusing on saving for something important."

- **Hack #563: Friend and Family Talk Practice**

It's okay to tell loved ones when you can't afford something — or don't want to prioritize it.

- **Hack #564: Limit Temptation Zones**

Unfollow, unsubscribe, or mute brands and shops that push you to overspend.

- **Hack #565: Permission to Disappoint**

You're allowed to disappoint people sometimes to take care of yourself. Guilt ≠ obligation.

Financial Wins = Mental Health Wins – Why Every Step Matters

Every dollar saved, every debt payment made, every mindful spending choice isn't just a financial win — it's a mental health upgrade too.

This section helps you reframe progress in a way that keeps motivation (and emotional energy) flowing.

- **Hack #566: Track the Emotional Wins**

Notice and name how financial progress makes you *feel* better — calmer, stronger, freer.

- **Hack #567: Celebrate Calm, Not Just Cash**

Saving $100 feels good. But so does sleeping better because you aren't stressing over bills.

- **Hack #568: Emotional ROI Journals**

Keep a journal of how money moves improve your daily emotional state. It's way more motivating than just tracking numbers.

- **Hack #569: Tiny Wins Matter Most**

The tiny, boring wins (packed lunches, skipped splurges, paid bills) build your emotional resilience.

- **Hack #570: Mental Wealth Over Net Worth**

A calmer, happier mind is the real flex — not just a bigger bank balance.

Conclusion: Your Wins Are Already in Motion

You made it — not just to the end of this book, but to the beginning of something better.

You're not standing at the starting line anymore. **You're moving.** Quietly, steadily, stubbornly building a life that doesn't run on panic or luck — it runs on *momentum.* Real financial wins aren't about sudden breakthroughs or perfect spreadsheets. **They're built from moments just like this**: where you show up for yourself, even when it would have been easier not to.

Shortcut Society isn't about hustling harder. It's about living smarter. It's about understanding that success is built in small, sneaky, brilliant ways — the everyday moves most people overlook.

You've learned to **save without feeling miserable.** To **spend with joy, not guilt.** To **bounce back after setbacks** instead of getting stuck. To **treat money like a tool you control**, not a mystery that controls you.

That's not luck. That's not magic. **That's skill — a skill you've already started building, one shortcut at a time.**

From here, your wins won't always look flashy. Some days, your progress might be loud — *paying off a debt, hitting a savings goal, negotiating a bill like a boss.* Other days, it might look quiet — *checking your account without anxiety, saying no to a pointless splurge, or choosing to reset after a rough month.*

Both kinds of wins matter. **Both are momentum. Both mean you're still moving.**

There will be setbacks. *That's not failure — that's life.* There will be boring days. *That's not failure either — that's how real success feels before it shows up in big ways.*

The Shortcut Society mindset is simple:

- Keep moving forward, even when it's slow.
- Reset quickly after mistakes, without shame.
- Celebrate every step — because every step counts.

You don't have to be perfect. You don't have to catch up to anyone else's timeline. **You just have to stay in motion — one tiny, stubborn, unstoppable step at a time.**

Momentum will do the rest.

This isn't the end of your money story. It's the part where you stop surviving and start designing.

A life with fewer regrets.A life with more breathing room.**A life where money stops being a source of stress and starts being a source of strength.**

That's what you're building now.**That's what you're already doing.**

And trust me — *Future You?* **They're already throwing confetti.**

Shortcut Society isn't something you read about.**It's something you live.**Starting today.Starting right now.

Let's go.

www.ingramcontent.com/pod-product-compliance
Lightning Source LLC
Chambersburg PA
CBHW052101070526
44584CB00017B/2286